ISLAM IN THE CIS

The Central Asian and Caucasian Prospects project is sponsored by:

- BG plc
- BP
- Shell International Petroleum Company Ltd
- Statoil

Series editor: Edmund Herzig
Head, Russia and Eurasia Programme: Roy Allison

ISLAM IN THE CIS
A Threat to Stability?

Yaacov Ro'i

THE ROYAL INSTITUTE OF
INTERNATIONAL AFFAIRS
Russia and Eurasia Programme

Published in Great Britain in 2001 by the Royal Institute of International Affairs,
Chatham House, 10 St James's Square, London SW1Y 4LE
(Charity Registration No. 208 223)

Distributed worldwide by the Brookings Institution, 1775 Massachusetts Avenue, NW
Washington, DC 20036-2188, USA

ISBN 1 86203 115 0

Typeset in Times by Koinonia, Manchester
Printed and bound in Great Britain by the Chameleon Press Limited
Cover design by Youngs Design in Production

CONTENTS

About the author vii

Acknowledgments viii

Abbreviations ix

Glossary x

Summary xii

1   The legacy of the past 1

2   The impact of *glasnost* on Soviet Islam 4

3   The Islamic revival after the break-up of the Soviet Union 10
    The return to pre-Soviet Islam 10
    Religiosity 12
    Mosque construction 15
    Education 16
    The status of women and gender relations 19
    Literature 21
    Summary 22

4   The politicization of Islam 24
    The perception of the threat 25
    Islamic movements and parties 28
    Islam and secular parties and movements 34
    An Islamic state? The case of Chechnya 36
    Political Islam as a threat to law and order 39

5   Regional attributes and differences 41
    Tajikistan 41
    Uzbekistan 42
    Dagestan 43
    Chechnya 47
    Kazakhstan 47
    Tatarstan 49
    Summary 50

6   Governments and Islam 51

7   Islamic solidarity 62
    Within the CIS 62
    The Muslim world outside 64

8   Under what circumstances might Islam threaten stability? 73
    The lessons of Tashkent, February 1999 73
    Batken, August–September 1999 75
    The second Chechen war 77
    The second Batken crisis and the incursion into Uzbekistan, August 2000 78
    Summary 81

9   Conclusion 83

Further reading 86

ABOUT THE AUTHOR

Yaacov Ro'i is professor of history at Tel Aviv University and senior research fellow there at the Cummings Center for Russian and East European Studies. He has published a number of works on Soviet Central Asia and Islam, including two edited volumes – *The USSR and the Muslim World* (George Allen & Unwin, 1984); and *Muslim Eurasia: Conflicting Legacies* (Frank Cass, 1995) – and one monograph, *Islam in the Soviet Union from the Second World War to Gorbachev* (Christopher Hurst and Columbia University Press, 2000).

ACKNOWLEDGMENTS

I am deeply indebted to Roy Allison and Edmund Herzig of the Royal Institute of International Affairs for their support and assistance throughout the preparation of this study. It has been a pleasure and a privilege to work with them. I am also grateful to the participants in a Chatham House Study Group for their comments on the first draft of this study; some of them even followed up with valuable contributions which I have incorporated and acknowledged. Finally, I wish to thank Vladimir Babak, Deena Leventer and Alon Winer of the Cummings Center for Russian and East European Studies at Tel Aviv University, who gave me their time and advice without so much as a murmur.

August 2001   Y.R.

ABBREVIATIONS

ASSR	Autonomous Soviet Socialist Republic
CIS	Commonwealth of Independent States
CP	Communist Party
CPSU	Communist Party of the Soviet Union
CRA	Council for Religious Affairs
DUMD	Spiritual Administration of the Muslims of Dagestan
DUMES	Spiritual Administration of the Muslims of European Russia and Siberia (until 1948 known as TsDUM)
DUMSK	Spiritual Administration of the Muslims of Northern Caucasus
GUAM	Georgia, Ukraine, Azerbaijan, Moldova grouping
IMU	Islamic Movement of Uzbekistan
IPA	Islamic Party of Azerbaijan
IRM	Islamic Revival Movement
IRP	Islamic Revival Party
IRPT	Islamic Revival Party of Tajikistan
PRM	Party of Russian Muslims
RSFSR	Russian Soviet Federal Socialist Republic
RUM	Russian Union of Muslims
SADUM	Spiritual Administration of the Muslims of Central Asia and Kazakhstan
UTO	United Tajik Opposition
VDP	Vainakh Democratic Party

GLOSSARY

adat	local or tribal custom
aksakal	elder (lit. white beard)
ghazavat	holy war (North Caucasus); religious war against the infidel to liberate Muslim lands from non-Muslim yoke
hajj	annual pilgrimage to Mecca and Medina; one of Islam's Five Pillars
hijab	headscarf worn by Muslim women in certain regions
imam	prayer-leader (Sunni), one who stands in front of the congregation
imam-khatib	imam who also fills the role of *khatib*, i.e. delivers the Friday sermon, the *khutba*
ishan	Sufi teacher or leader (Central Asia)
jamaat	community (North Caucasus)
jihad	holy war (see *ghazavat*)
khatib	see *imam-khatib*
khutba	Friday sermon by the *khatib*
madhhab	Islamic doctrinal school
madrasa	advanced religious school
mahalla	neighbourbood of traditional urban settlement (Central Asia)
mufti	head of Muslim spiritual directorate (Russia/Soviet Union/CIS)
mujahid(in)	person who takes part in a *jihad*; used in Afghanistan for Muslims who opposed the Marxist regime that took power in 1978 and the Soviet invasion
murid	Sufi novice or adept
otyn	female religious figure who gives religious instruction to girls and performs religious rites for women
paranja	garment covering a woman from head to foot
qazi (qadi)	person who sits in judgment in Islamic court; in Central Asia learned theologian who interprets *Shari'a* law, sometimes used for representative of Spiritual Administration; in North Caucasus, religious figure in mosque
qazi kalon	head *qazi*, head of religious establishment (Tajikistan)
salafiyya/salafi	movement for return to the golden age of Islam's first four khalifs

Shari'a	Muslim code of law
tariqat	brotherhood
ulama	religious scholar
umma	universal community of Islam, embracing all believers
waqf	religious endowment
Wahhabi	adherent of sect founded in eighteenth century in Arabian Peninsula for return to pure Islam; loosely used to denote all Islamic radicals and fundamentalists (Soviet Union/CIS)
wird	sub-division of Sufi *tariqat* or brotherhood
zikr, dhikr	integral part of ritual of Sufi and dervish orders
ziyarat	Muslim shrine (North Caucasus)

SUMMARY

Islam has become an important topic of debate in the Soviet successor states with significant ethnic Muslim populations. These comprise the five Central Asian states – Kazakhstan, Kyrgyzstan, Tajikistan, Turkmenistan and Uzbekistan; Azerbaijan in the South Caucasus; and the Russian Federation, which includes a number of Muslim ethnic republics – Tatarstan and Bashkortostan in the Middle Volga and the North Caucasian republics of Chechnya, Dagestan, Ingushetia, Kabardino-Balkaria and Karachaevo-Cherkessia.

Given, on the one hand, the overlap of religion and nationalism and consequently of the religious revival and the nascent national movements throughout the former Soviet Union, and, on the other hand, the loaded nature of political Islam and its identification in the West with international terror in the last decades of the twentieth century, the new regimes have sought to associate Islam and political opposition and to depict the former as potentially subversive.

This has had different implications in Russia and in those states where the titular nationality is traditionally Muslim. In Russia, portraying Islam as a threat to the stability and security of both state and society was culturally and psychologically acceptable, to the point of being likely to win considerable popular support. In the Muslim states, however, it meant creating a divide between those who identified with the values of modernity and secularism as the principal criteria for constructing their new nation-states and those, including the Islamists, who sought to focus rather on cultural specificity and traditions.

This dichotomy has acquired different dimensions and proportions in the various states under study. Yet, on the whole, against the backdrop of regimes with a marked tendency for authoritarianism, it seems to have been conducive to a greater religious and political radicalization of the Islamists and in some instances to have made them bedfellows of marginal social and political groups. The end result has been a growing polarization between Islamic groups, parties and organizations and the authorities, who – having preached the theory of an Islamic threat for some years in order to legitimize their own policies – began in the years 1999 and 2000 to encounter the first indications that such a threat to their regimes might indeed materialize.

As of the time of writing, the challenge has been tenuous. It has, at the same time, posed a major question which this study seeks to address – namely, how far do the preconditions exist for such a threat to become serious? This could occur if the Islamists themselves gained strength and acquired new resources. Or it could come about if opportunities presented themselves for the Islamists to convince significant strata among the population that a threat to the ruling elite emanating from Islam does not endanger the well-being of the wider society, which might rather be threatened in the long run by the dominant regimes. This study contends that as long as the resilience of the regimes remains unimpaired, such a contingency is unlikely, but were it to weaken for one reason or another, Islam might well surface as a viable alternative.

Many features of post-Soviet Islam that are common to the states of the CIS were also characteristic of other Muslim countries when they sought to construct new political entities in the early years of independence from colonial rule. Moreover, it is inevitable that trends and developments in the Muslim world in more recent years have been influencing the new Muslim states of the CIS as well as Russia's Muslim regions. This study does not, however, make comparisons with the situation in Muslim countries in North Africa, the Middle East or South and Southeast Asia, or with the situation regarding other faiths in the CIS, which have undergone processes similar to those that have affected Islam in the context of the disintegration of the Soviet Union. Abstention from even a superficial treatment of these issues does not imply that the author regards them as irrelevant; rather, the framework of this study does not lend itself to such a discussion.

1 THE LEGACY OF THE PAST

The disintegration of the Soviet Union and its replacement by fifteen successor states in late 1991 did not mean a fresh start in the former Soviet territory. Much remained from the past – personalities, perceptions, institutions. Just as the October Revolution of 1917, despite being heralded as the great break with the country's tsarist past, inherited a great deal along with all that it created *ex nihilo,* so too did the new, independent 'nation-states'. Perhaps in no sphere was this historical continuum more conspicuous than in the central authorities' perception of Islam and its role in society.

Imperial Russia had looked upon Islam as a potential threat to Holy Russia's special role within Christendom and European civilization. One of the justifications for Russia's role as a great power was its geostrategic position between Europe and Asia. Islam's traditional aggressiveness, which had in the course of history expressed itself in attacks upon the West's more exposed peripheries, would henceforth be held at bay by St Petersburg. In the domestic arena too the Imperial Court devised different methods for ensuring that the territories and peoples Russia conquered in its wars against the various Muslim khanates along the Volga, in Siberia and, later, in Central Asia and against the Persian and Ottoman empires would not undermine its authority. To this end, Islam had to be tamed and subordinated; its inherent perils and hazards, which might at any time endanger the integrity, indeed essence, of the Romanov empire, had to be eliminated.

From time to time in its very early years the Bolshevik regime made gestures of rapprochement towards the USSR's Muslim populations. But, although the whole-sale repression of Islam began later than the persecution of other religions, by the time of the Second World War it too had been truncated and enfeebled throughout the Soviet Union. The only perceptible pockets of religion that remained were in some of the more outlying and inaccessible regions of the North Caucasus and Central Asia. When during the war the Soviet leadership made its peace with the Russian Orthodox Church and then with other religious hierarchies in order to ensure the loyalty of believer communities to the Soviet war effort, it recreated the Muslim spiritual directorates.[1] These became, as they had been under the tsars, collaborators with a

---

[1] Under the tsars, at least since the establishment by Catherine the Great of the Orenburg Muhammedan Spiritual Assembly in 1788, spiritual directorates had enabled the central government to supervise and

regime which most fervent believers viewed, not without reason, as the arch-enemy of Islam. In this way a major, almost unsurmountable, barrier was formed between establishment Islam and at least some elements within non-establishment, 'parallel' Islam. True, the weight of popular or folk Islam was in many regions clearly preponderant. Its leaders, Sufi *ishans* in Central Asia and the mentors of Sufi *wirds* in the Caucasus, continued to enjoy much prestige among their followers. This applied especially to rural regions, where most of the indigenous population resided. The repositories of Islam there often seemed to be on the one hand the plenteous local shrines and, on the other hand, social occasions – funerals and memorial services, circumcisions and weddings – that retained a semi-religious character and that no communist propaganda or government repression was able to eliminate.

Although it followed developments and trends within the Soviet Muslim community, as well as other faiths, throughout the postwar period, the Soviet regime did not anticipate any serious danger from it. Nonetheless, in the 1960s and early 1970s some 'extremist' Muslims were adopting 'anti-Soviet' or 'anti-social' positions, demanding the abolition of equality of rights for women and calling upon believers to refuse to serve in the Soviet armed forces or to let their children join the Pioneers or the Komsomol.

The regime's policy changed radically at the end of the 1970s, as a result of events in neighbouring Iran and Afghanistan. The Khomeini revolution brought to power a regime that committed itself to the dissemination of Islamic propaganda in the Soviet Union, while in Afghanistan the *mujahidin* declared war on the new Marxist-Leninist government. In the 1970s too, the more traditionally intransigent centres of Islamic activity within the USSR – the Fergana Valley and Tajikistan in Central Asia and Dagestan in the North Caucasus – began to show signs of initiating an Islamic revival, in contrast to the Chechen-Ingush ASSR, where antagonism to Moscow had focused on Islam since the return of the Chechen and Ingush peoples from deportation.[2] Once again, as under the tsars, Islam came to be perceived as likely to threaten the political order, and between 1981 and 1987 the Communist Party of the Soviet Union (CPSU)

---

control Muslim religious activity. The only such directorate to survive in 1917 was the original one, renamed that year the Central Spiritual Directorate of the Muslims of Inner Russia and Siberia (TsDUM); this became DUMES in 1948. A few short-lived directorates were set up in the mid-1920s, but well before the outbreak of war they had all disappeared, and again only TsDUM remained. In 1943 the Spiritual Directorate of the Muslims of Central Asia and Kazakhstan (SADUM) was formed, followed a year later by two further directorates, for the Muslims of the North Caucasus and of Transcaucasia (DUMSK and DUMZ).

[2] The Chechen and the Ingush had been among the 'punished peoples' deported by Stalin *en masse* to Kazakhstan and Central Asia during the Second World War. They were generally considered the most, or among the most, religiously oriented of all the Soviet Union's Muslim ethnic groups. Although they were allowed to return to their national patrimony in early 1957, it was not until 1979 that the first mosque was officially registered in the Chechen-Ingush ASSR.

Central Committee for the first time issued a number of resolutions relating specifically to Islam. They addressed the various aspects of this threat and sought to implement countermeasures. Although the texts of these resolutions have not been published, the contemporary literature clearly suggests the party leadership contended that Western imperialism was using Soviet Islam to undermine the stability of the country. It is certainly possible that the backdrop to this position was the protracted, resolute and largely successful struggle conducted by the Afghan *mujahidin* against not only the Afghan regime but also the Soviet forces which had invaded Afghanistan in December 1979 and remained there until 1989. And even if the threat to stability was not the official apologia, it must surely have had an indirect influence on the Soviet leadership's decision-making.

When Gorbachev came to power in 1985 he maintained this position. The harshness of his policy towards Islam was highlighted by a speech he delivered to the Uzbekistan CP Central Committee in November 1986. Its essential message, published as a major article the following May under the title 'Islam and Politics',[3] was that Islam was no longer in the category of a mere religion, which entailed in itself a danger to the ruling ideology, but had taken on political substance in a country where the sole permitted political institution was the CPSU. A condition of war existed thereafter between Islam and the Soviet government.

[3] Igor Beliaev, 'Islam i politika', *Literaturnaia gazeta*, 13 and 20 May 1987.

2 THE IMPACT OF GLASNOST ON SOVIET ISLAM

The processes and transformations that were the consequence of *glasnost* and *perestroika* also affected the USSR's Muslim areas. They arrived there somewhat later than elsewhere and made their mark rather more gingerly, yet there too informal organizations came into being, some of the old administrative personnel were replaced and the monopoly of power of the Communist Party was questioned. Demonstrations and disturbances became more commonplace – a few had occurred before, such as the anti-Russian demonstrations that had followed a soccer match at Pakhtakor stadium in Tashkent in 1969 and rocked the Uzbek elite. But now they were larger, more frequent and, above all, documented, for it was no longer possible to sweep them under the carpet.

Many of the activities that took place under the impact of *glasnost* and *perestroika* in the Muslim regions were wholly secular in nature; so were most of the informal associations which sprang up. At the same time, the Islamic revival that had begun in the previous decade benefited too. It became possible to build new mosques in large numbers as restrictions on their registration were gradually lifted, and where they remained they were usually not enforced. Religious education also became possible – previously it had been strictly prohibited and had persisted only clandestinely among the more devout Muslim populations of Dagestan, Tajikistan and some parts of the Fergana Valley. This education was a *sine qua non* for any meaningful religious awakening and activity and *madrasas* began opening in different parts of the country. Islamic literature began appearing too; for the most part it was imported or smuggled in from neighbouring and other Middle Eastern countries. Finally, while anti-Islamic invective persisted in the Soviet media, there were occasional indications that more perceptive commentators were having doubts as to the wisdom of a manifest anti-Islamic position. Some journals, notably *Ogonek*, were even opening up as forums for the expression of Muslim viewpoints, including non-conformist ones.

Against this background it was hardly surprising that Muslim organizations surfaced. Some of these were charitable in nature – charity had long been excluded from the sphere of legitimate religious activity on the grounds that in the Soviet Union there were no needy people. Others also started out as non-political but changed tack as soon as circumstances permitted. Sometimes an organization that was officially secular added Islamic overtones. This held especially for nationalist groups or movements: the overlap between ethnic cultural tradition and religion was one of the widely accepted assumptions of the nationalist renascence that took place in the Soviet Union in the 1960s and subsequent decades. (This was true first and foremost of the Russian nationalist movement, but it applied to its counterparts in most of the fifteen republics.)

Before the end of the 1980s, however, purely religious movements were applying to register. At first these were at local or, at most, at republic level, but in 1990 an All-Union Islamic Revival Party (IRP) was established in Astrakhan. It had antecedents in a number of informal groups that had come into being in different parts of the country, particularly in the Fergana Valley, Tajikistan and Dagestan. Here was a party that did not conceal its political goals, that refused to disguise its religious aims and that combined its Islamic and its political content. The appeal 'to the Muslims of the Soviet Union' which accompanied the party's programme pointed out that the spiritual directorates, 'limited in their activity as state organs, are compelled to engage solely in questions of a religious and ritual character'. If they did not actively participate in the country's political life, Muslims would not be able to 'realize their rights and take their rightful place in the life of society'. Prior to the establishment of the IRP, its programme contended, no political organization had defended Muslim rights, and that was the reason the party was now coming into existence. Against the background of prevalent Muslim disunity,

> we, Muslims of different nationalities and regions, and of different *madhhabs*, have resolved to unite in a single Islamic Revival Party with the purpose of disseminating Islam, consolidating the ties between all the Muslim peoples [of the Soviet Union], protecting the rights of Muslims at all levels, raising the political awareness of the Muslim masses, and defending their economic and other interests.

Indeed, the programme declared the necessity of regulating the economy on the basis of the *Shari'a* (Islamic law).

The programme went on to condemn 'ideas of national specificity' and declared that 'all Muslims comprise a single Islamic consociation (*soobshchestvo*), the *umma*'. At the same time, the programme supported the sovereignty of each people, upholding its right to choose the form of government that conformed to 'its traditions and spiritual values'. It also condemned 'extremism, terrorism and all forms of discrimination, kindling interethnic dissension and introducing martial law in the Muslim regions'. All problems were to be resolved without delay through 'competent, impartial and independent commissions'.[1] (The condemnation of 'extremism' and 'terrorism' clearly referred to oppression by the Soviet state.)

[1] 'Programma i ustav Islamskoi Partii Vozrozhdeniia', n.d.

The IRP, however, was never registered. Its founding conference was curtailed by the authorities; and although it succeeded in electing a leadership representing Muslims in various parts of the country, the party, insofar as it functioned at all, did so only through branches at the republic level (see Chapter 4).[2]

The failure of the all-union party to obtain registration demonstrated the limitations of *glasnost* and democratization with regard to Islam. The idea of Islam obtaining political instruments which might enable it to compete on a par with other constituencies in the new multi-party body politic was clearly anathema to the helmsmen of the 'new' ship of state.[3]

In Uzbekistan in particular, the new Communist Party First Secretary, Islam Karimov, who had succeeded Rafik Nishanov in summer 1989, did not hesitate to make clear his own position on Islam and politics. Addressing the party leadership within months of his appointment, he said that 'freedom of conscience does not mean freedom to ignore state laws and to teach intolerance and hatred on a religious basis, as is being done by individual sects holding extremist views'.[4] Karimov was manifestly alluding to Muslim groups which the security forces and the media had been indiscriminately calling Wahhabis for some years and which some sources insinuated had been responsible for the Fergana Valley disturbances of May–June 1989, in which Uzbeks perpetrated pogroms against Meskhetian Turks in a number of towns and rural regions.[5] Having come to power in the immediate wake of these events, Karimov had every reason to stress stability as the slogan of his rule. From the very start, he highlighted the role of the Communist Party as 'the chief factor of stabilization, the chief obstacle ... to antisocial forces'[6] and took measures to restrict civil rights.[7] In this context political Islam had little chance indeed.

It was not only in Uzbekistan that the leadership interpreted *glasnost* in a way that appeared to contradict its essential meaning; there were signs of a similar trend at the centre as well. Officials of the Council for Religious Affairs (CRA), the government body responsible for monitoring developments among the country's various religious communities, had long been reporting the dangers to the Soviet regime of the Sufi *tariqats* (orders or brotherhoods) in the North Caucasus, notably in the Chechen-

---

[2] Perhaps the most authentic account of the IRP's formation and its failure to influence the political arena outside Tajikistan is that by one of its founding members, Valiakhmet Sadur, '"Islamskii faktor": zametki i razmyshleniia russkogo musul'manina', *Dia-Logos* (Moscow), 1997, pp. 224–36. For further detail concerning the IRPT after independence, see Chapter 4.

[3] For Gorbachev's position regarding Islam, see Chapter 1.

[4] *Pravda vostoka*, 25 November 1989.

[5] Tashkent Obkom Secretary E.I. Fazylov referred in this context to Wahhabis, whom he called 'warriors for the purity of Islam', in an interview he gave to *Nauka i religiia*, 11, 1989, p. 13, implying that Islam in Uzbekistan was under their influence.

[6] *Pravda vostoka*, 4 January 1990.

[7] *Pravda vostoka*, 11 February 1990.

Ingush ASSR but also in Dagestan and the North Ossetian Republic. They continued in the Gorbachev period to dwell on the features of Sufism (usually referred to in Soviet sources as *muridism,* after the *murids* or disciples of Sufi religious leaders) which seemed to undermine the stability of Soviet society and the authority of Soviet institutions in these areas. Those features were in particular the Sufis' 'organizational and ideological seclusion, their subordination to Muslim authorities and their peculiar religious ritual, especially the *zikr'.* At the same time, the CRA suggested breaking with the traditional condemnation of Sufi groups as sects, which in Soviet terminology placed them *a priori* beyond the pale of legality, and somehow bringing them into the fold of official orthodox Islam.[8]

An analysis in 1989 of 'the socio-political orientation of Muslim religious associations in the RSFSR' pointed out that Islam as a world religion had become politicized in the twentieth century because 'the foundations of the faith stood in contradiction to the political and socio-economic requirements of Muslim society'. Islam's 'ideologues' therefore had to make its institutions conform to the development of society, to modernize and to link the faith to the process of scientific and technological progress. In the Soviet Union the Muslim religious establishment had conducted itself loyally since the Second World War, and the clergy for the most part accepted the implications of *glasnost* and *perestroika* and the current trends of Soviet policy. Here and there, however, there were a few signs of trouble. These included religious figures' and believers' identification of Muslim with national tradition; complaints that the state discriminated against Islam – these had occurred in particular in the wake of Gorbachev's rapprochement with the Russian Orthodox Church and the festivities surrounding the millennium of Christianity in Russia but had been mitigated after the celebration of the 200th anniversary of the Spiritual Administration of the Muslims of European Russia and Siberia (DUMES); and occasional exploitation of the new freedoms to hold political meetings in a religious context. But on the whole, it seemed that general trends were of a positive nature, and as long as officialdom conducted its affairs effectively and thoughtfully, Islam could be expected to abide by the rules set down by the secular power.[9]

The same analysis concluded, however, that the North Caucasus continued to be a cause of concern. 'Destabilizing elements' had initiated 'extremist actions', causing antagonism on religious and ethnic lines. A number of religious activists were uniting around a platform which essentially confirmed Islam's traditional institutions as

---

[8] 'Analytical report on Muridism and measures for neutralizing its negative influence', sent by RSFSR CRA Chairman L.F. Kolesnikov to the Yaroslavl' Oblispolkom, 5 May 1989 – Gosudarstvennyi Arhkiv Rossiiskoi Federatsii (GARF) – the State Archive of the Russian Federation, f.R-1033, o.1, d.101, ll.12–21; document in possession of the Keston Institute, Oxford, as are those mentioned in notes 9 and 10.

[9] This report too was sent by Kolesnikov to the Yaroslavl' Oblispolkom, 12 December 1989 – GARF, f.R-1033, o.1, d.101, ll. 63–79.

obligatory norms of contemporary Muslim life. This led them to adopt the political practice of 'Muslim fundamentalism', undertaking to Islamize society and to sanction the use of force to achieve its goals. Misinterpreting the extension of democracy and *glasnost* as permissiveness, they proceeded to organize all kinds of unsanctioned public activity – meetings, ultimatums and so on. They made common cause with informal groups and attracted to their ranks the intelligentsia, women and even children. The activity of the North Caucasians linked up with that of religious fundamentalists in Central Asia, from whom some of them had received instruction. One CRA official saw a clear link between the demonstrations that had led to the ousting of the mufti of SADUM in Tashkent in February 1989 and those that had induced the removal of the mufti of the Spiritual Administration of the Muslims of Northern Caucasus (DUMSK) in Makhachkala, the capital of Dagestan, three months later. Indeed, the organizers of the meeting in Buinaksk that had preceded the demonstrations in the Dagestani capital had spoken of their intention to set up an Islamic republic.

In Dagestan 'informals' were actively advocating the formation of an Islamic party, nationalists were seeking to use clergy and believers to promote their goals and religious figures were in contact with 'the so-called national front'. It was therefore incumbent upon the administration to do all in its power to separate religious and nationalist elements. Islam in the Chechen-Ingush ASSR had long been linked with Islam in Dagestan, but now the clergy in the former were seeking to set up their own religious centre and formations. This was encouraged by the CRA, for the alternative seemed to be to hand over the religious leadership to a group of people led by Wahhabis who supported the positions of fellow fanatics in Dagestan.[10]

There can be little doubt that those among the bureaucracy who studied the situation in the North Caucasus were well aware that the hard line followed by Moscow's representatives in the region had given religious figures an excellent pretext to reject their authority. Perhaps it even provided them with little alternative. (In Dagestan not a single religious association had been registered for over twenty years, and more than 100 applications to register were pending.)

Islam under Gorbachev was inevitably influenced by *glasnost* and *perestroika*, and religious leaders and ordinary believers sought to take advantage of the new climate to expand their activities. These included participating in the political life of the USSR, in which the CPSU was no longer the sole source of power. On the all-union level and in those parts where republican and local bureaucracies were prepared to countenance these activities and initiatives and/or were relatively sophisticated they proceeded to evolve for the most part without causing waves.

---

[10] Minutes, Conference of workers of CRA apparatus in North Caucasus and of their meeting with leaders of the region's Muslim religious centres, Groznyi, 16–17 April 1990 and information on the results of the conference – f.R-1033, o.1, d.106, ll. 40–54 and 65–8.

Elsewhere, where officialdom was more obdurate, the Islamists, insofar as they were intent on achieving their goals, were compelled to be more extreme. This applied in particular to those areas that had a history of a strong anti-establishment Islam, notably the Fergana Valley and Tajikistan in Central Asia and Dagestan and the Chechen-Ingush ASSR. But whether a more radical Islam provoked more restrictive measures on the part of the authorities or whether the latter's greater intransigence bred a more virulent Islam is difficult to determine. Certainly, the two trends seem to have nurtured each other both in the earlier Soviet period and in the Gorbachev years.

3 THE ISLAMIC REVIVAL AFTER THE BREAK-UP OF THE SOVIET UNION

The momentum of the later Gorbachev period with regard to the Islamic revival continued into the first years after the break-up of the Soviet Union. It soon became evident, however, that the various governments concerned – those of the Russian Federation and the six Muslim successor states – responded rather differently to religion in general and to Islam in particular. The heterogeneity of these countries' political atmospheres, in addition to long-standing regional differences, meant that the dynamics of this revival differed considerably from one state to another and from region to region within the states (see Chapter 5). Nonetheless, a number of general trends were noticeable. Some were common to the Islamic revival in other Muslim countries; others were specific to the Soviet Union/CIS. The former included an emphasis on social justice as an Islamic value and a sense that Islamic values should be applied in treating social, economic and political issues; an extension of participation in religious discourse so as to embrace those who were not religious professionals or specialists; the claim of contenders for power that they represented true Islam, whereas their opponents were un-Islamic; and an insistence that over the centuries Islam had been corrupted by a series of religious and secular leaders.[1] Other trends were first and foremost a reaction to developments connected specifically with the Soviet experience, which the Islamists were resolved to undo, but they often converged with general, universal trends.

The return to pre-Soviet Islam

Islamic figures and movements, in their endeavour to shake off the shackles imposed by communism, took an interest in the nature of Islam in the Russian empire, just as national intelligentsias attempted to assert their national identity and to recover the treasures of their ethnic cultures which they felt the Soviet regime had suppressed. It was not sufficient to be rid of some of the characteristic trappings of Soviet Islam, notably the establishment that had collaborated with a regime which had denounced religion and made major efforts to eradicate it. It was also necessary to try to resuscitate

---

[1] Edmund Herzig, 'Islam, Transnationalism and Subregionalism in the CIS', in Renata Dwan and Oleksandr Pavliuk (eds), *Building Security in the New States of Eurasia* (Armonk, NY: East-West Institute and M.E. Sharpe, 2000), pp. 229–30.

some of the trends which had begun to influence Islam in the last decades of the Russian Empire and to give it a life of its own.

The most important of these trends was Jadidism. This was a movement which in the decades prior to the October Revolution had undertaken the task of modernizing Islam in order to bring it into line with the scientific and technological revolutions that were altering the face of society. Beginning with education, it established schools that would enable young Muslims to take up secular studies together with religious ones (*usul al-jadid*). Jadidism introduced a totally new social ethos. Indeed, it challenged the hold of the conservative clergy on the community and sought to show the compatibility of Islam and modernization. Secularization, its leaders contended, did not of necessity mean becoming worse Muslims, let alone shedding Islam altogether. Many of those members of the Muslim nations who had affiliated themselves with reformist and socialist parties in the years following the 1905 revolution and with the Bolsheviks after 1917 were Jadidists who believed that these movements would alleviate the lot of the Muslims and of Islam.[2] The heart of their message, the national liberation of the empire's Muslim ethnic groups, was clearly relevant in the early 1990s as these same groups attained independence or, in the case of those remaining in the Russian Federation, upgraded their national status. Islamic figures at the end of the twentieth century felt and even highlighted the continuity between the tasks and goals of the Jadidists and their own aims. The books and pamphlets of the former were reprinted and their ideas addressed and developed in newspapers and journals. A new organization came into being, calling itself the Jadid Party of Uzbekistan. Abduwali Mirzoyev, one of the leading figures of the Islamic revival in that republic, when asked about the main tasks of the Muslim community in independent Uzbekistan, spoke of the necessity of being flexible in renovating society and revising certain traditions and of reintroducing mixed religious and secular education.[3] The All-Tatar Public Centre's programme for 1991, which included a section entitled 'Islam in Tatar Society', likewise considered the revival of the 'salutary traditions of Jadidism' to be one of the movement's assignments.[4]

Although the slogans of Jadidism had seemed crucial and rational to certain sections of the Muslim intelligentsia in the last decades of the Russian empire, the movement met with considerable opposition within the Muslim community. Its opponents were called *qadimists*, those who sought to preserve traditional structures

[2] For the Jadid movement, see Adeeb Khalid, *The Politics of Muslim Cultural Reform: Jadidism in Central Asia* (Berkeley and Los Angeles: University of California Press, 1998).

[3] Abdujabbar A. Abduvakhitov, 'The Jadid Movement and Its Impact on Contemporary Central Asia', in Hafeez Malik (ed.), *Central Asia: Its Strategic Importance and Future Prospects* (New York: St Martin's Press, 1994), pp. 65–75.

[4] Rafik Mukhametshin, *Islam v obshchestvenno-politicheskoi zhizni Tatarstana v kontse XX veka* (Kazan': Iman, 2000), pp. 60–1.

and perceptions in order not to undermine Islam's hold on society. As the Islamic revival took shape in the 1980s and 1990s, many of its central figures likewise rejected the political and social assumptions of the heirs of Jadidism. Nor, however, did they adhere to the teachings and practices of establishment Islam under the Soviet regime, which was formally the heir of the conservative clergy of the nineteenth century although many of its positions were closer to those of the Jadidists. These Islamists called instead for a return to primordial Islam, for a rejection of the additions made to Islamic doctrine and dogma over the centuries. This was no new position; such calls had been made for hundreds of years. It was not even a new position in Central Asia, where some *ulamas* (religious scholars), for example in the Kokand Khanate, had initiated reform in the mid-eighteenth century under the banner of a return to the pure Islam of the Prophet and his four successors (the four rightly guided caliphs).[5] In the late nineteenth century the neo-orthodox brand of Islamic reformism that aimed to regenerate Islam by a return to the early traditions was called Salafiyya. In the post-Soviet era, as in the last years of the USSR, the adherents of Salafiyya became known as Wahhabis, after a movement that had come into being in Arabia in the eighteenth century with the general aim of doing away with all innovations to Islam after the third century of its existence. The Wahhabis belonged to the Hanbali *madhhab* and continued to comprise the leading school in Saudi Islam in the twentieth century.[6]

This return to models that had existed a century or so previously did not recreate the situation that had pertained on the eve of the October Revolution. Nor, indeed, could it do so, for the political and social environment was dissimilar in many ways. Yet there was once again a major divide in Islam between 'fundamentalists', whose main objective was to strengthen Islam from within by purifying it of extraneous and peripheral influences, and those whose principal concern was its legitimization and social and political recovery.

Religiosity

Regional differences continued to be central in all that concerned religiosity, just as they had been in the Soviet period.[7] Those areas where religious practice was intense in the past have retained this inclination since independence, and areas where the

[5] Bakhtiyar Babadzhanov, 'The Fergana Valley: Source or Victim of Islamic Fundamentalism?', in Lena Jonson and Murad Esenov (eds), *Political Islam and Conflicts in Russia and Central Asia* (Stockholm: The Swedish Institute of International Affairs, 1999), p. 113. The nineteenth-century American diplomat and traveller Eugene Schuyler referred specifically to a Wahhabi preacher in Kokand. Eugene Schuyler, *Turkestan* (London, 1876), vol. 2, p. 254.
[6] The reasons for this designation will be discussed in Chapter 4. See also Chapter 2.
[7] On religiosity in the Soviet period, see Y. Ro'i, *Islam in the Soviet Union* (London: Christopher Hurst/ New York: Columbia University Press, 2000), chs 7–9.

practice was less intense have remained the same. For instance, in Uzbekistan the Fergana Valley has retained its claim to be the focus of the most fervent religious activity, and in Kyrgyzstan the south remains manifestly more religious than the north; Muslims in the north and centre do not for the most part observe the Ramadan fast (the *uraz*) or perform the five daily prayers (the *salat* or *namaz*), although this fast is reportedly observed more widely than in the past, even in the towns. Practically all, however, celebrate the two major festivals, conduct funerals and weddings to the accompaniment of prayer and/or readings from the Qur'an, circumcise their sons and abstain from eating pork.[8] In other words, the removal of restrictions on Islamic practice has not been accompanied by any large-scale upward turn in performing the prescriptions of the faith, especially among older people and the urban intelligentsia. Even many of the younger people who seek a focus for their collective identity by turning to Islam do not seem to be fulfilling most of its precepts. (Identification with a religion without observing its rituals and precepts seems to be characteristic of many secular societies.)

Public opinion surveys in four of the new Muslim states revealed that in the mid-1990s one-half to three-quarters of the titular nationalities considered themselves to be believers, yet only a small percentage of professed believers observed their faith on a regular basis.[9] A survey conducted in 1996 revealed that in Tajikistan, where 97 per cent of the population designated themselves believers, 64 per cent did not pray at all, although in the older age brackets the picture was rather different – 67 per cent of the 65–74 age group prayed five times a day.[10] In early 2000, 90 per cent of the members of Muslim nationalities in Azerbaijan, 88 per cent in Tajikistan and 80 per cent in Kazakhstan declared themselves to be believers. Of these, two-thirds in Tajikistan affirmed that they observed at least three of the 'Five Pillars' of Islam, as against one-half in Uzbekistan and one-third in Kazakhstan.[11] (Differences in the wording of the questions and in the sample make it difficult to reach concrete conclusions about trends in religious observances since independence.)

[8] Anara Tabyshalieva, 'Vzgliad na religioznuiu situatsiiu v Kyrgyzstane', *Tsentral'naia Aziia*, no. 6 (12), 1997, p. 71.

[9] David Pollock and Elaine El Assad (eds), *In the Eye of the Beholder: Muslim and Non-Muslim Views of Islam, Islamic Politics and Each Other* (Washington, DC: USIA Office of Research and Media Reaction, August 1995), pp. 25 and 27.

[10] The survey results are given in Saodat Olimova, 'Political Islam and Conflict in Tajikistan', in Jonson and Esenov (eds), *Political Islam and Conflicts*, p. 128. See also Aleksandr Dzhumaev, 'Tsentral'naia Aziia: religiia i obshchestvo – tema ocherednogo seminara Fonda "Soros-Kyrygyzstan"', *Tsentral'naia Aziia*, no. 6 (12), 1997, p. 9.

[11] 'Central Asians Differ on Islam's Political Role, But Agree on a Secular State', US Department of State, Office of Research, Opinion Analysis, 6 July 2000, pp. 2 and 3 and Tables 5 and 7. (At least some of the data relating to Uzbekistan seem to the compilers of the report to be a serious underestimate, which they attribute to political circumstances.)

These findings notwithstanding, the very identification with Islam by large sectors of the population which did not identify with it at the end of the Soviet period does seem to indicate a certain re-Islamization of society that cannot be ignored. Its origins may be several – from the deterioration of the socio-economic situation and disappointment with the general, humanist slogans of *glasnost* and 'democratization' to an increasing conviction that Islamic values and customs are an integral component of the national culture. In some of the more intensely Muslim areas, the communist symbols and slogans of the Soviet period were quickly replaced by Muslim ones.[12] Public life in Dagestan, for instance, underwent a 'spontaneous Islamization', especially in rural areas.[13] Whatever its cause, which may well differ from one region to another, the trend is clear and must be taken to reflect a certain mood or atmosphere that will inevitably have social and political repercussions.[14]

Another indication of the re-Islamization of Muslim society is that two of the Five Pillars of Islam have enjoyed a revival, namely charity (*zakat*) and the pilgrimage (*hajj*). The Soviet regime proscribed both practices, the former because it could not acknowledge the prevalence of indigence among its citizenry (see Chapter 2), the latter because it was not prepared for more than a handful of carefully screened individuals to come into contact with masses of believing Muslims in Mecca and Medina at the Festival of the Sacrifice ('*Id al-adha*). The 1990s saw the revival of Muslim charitable organizations and institutions. The Muslim spiritual administrations or muftiates themselves undertook to provide help to pensioners, orphans and large families, and the mosques reverted to fulfilling their traditional charitable and social activities.[15] In the survey conducted in 2000, 87 per cent of Muslims in Kazakhstan, 81 per cent in Tajikistan and 72 per cent in Uzbekistan claimed they gave alms.[16]

The *hajj* has been undertaken by tens of thousands of Muslims from the various countries of the CIS. The number of pilgrims began to swell in the last two years of Gorbachev's rule and grew even more in the first two years after the Soviet Union's collapse, but then it began to decline because of inflation and the huge expenses involved.[17] This decline does not, however, seem to have occurred in all areas equally.

---

[12] V.O. Bobrovnikov, 'Islam i sovetskoe nasledie v kolkhozakh Severno-Zapadnogo Dagestana', *Etnograficheskoe obozrenie*, no. 5, 1997, p. 132.

[13] D.V. Makarov, *Ofitsial'nyi i neofitsial'nyi islam v Dagestane* (Moscow: Tsentr strategicheskikh i politicheskikh issledovanii, 2000), p. 5.

[14] For this trend in Tatarstan, see Mukhametshin, *Islam v obshchestvenno-politicheskoi zhizni Tatarstana*, pp. 85–7.

[15] Gasym Kerimov, 'Islam and Muslims in Russia since the Collapse of the Soviet Union', *Religion, State and Society* (henceforth *RSS*), vol. 24, no. 2/3 (September 1996), pp. 190–1.

[16] 'Central Asians Differ on Islam's Political Role', Table 5.

[17] Nevertheless, about 600 Muslims from Kazakhstan undertook the *hajj* in 1997 at their own expense. Some 200 Chechens resident in Kazakhstan, however, went on the pilgrimage at the expense of foreign Muslim centres. Iakov Trofimov, 'Sovremennaia religioznaia situatsiia v Respublike Kazakhstan', *Tsentral'naia Aziia*, no. 6 (12), 1997, p. 62. Only in Turkmenistan did the pilgrimage retain its Soviet

Thus, in the mid-1990s hundreds of buses took pilgrims from Dagestan to Saudi Arabia, and some 12,200 made the *hajj* from that republic in 1997 alone.[18]

Mosque construction

The number of mosques has grown enormously. This applies both to the larger, so-called Friday (*jum'a*) mosques and the smaller, community (*mahalla*) ones. In many cases, the distinction between the two categories has become blurred.[19] The large-scale opening of mosques began under *perestroika*, and gathered momentum after 1991. Not all the newly opened mosques were recent constructions: many in more remote areas had functioned more or less throughout the Soviet period without registration; others had been sequestrated in periods of repression, mostly in the 1930s, and were now restored to their original function. But there were many new buildings as well. In Uzbekistan, for example, where there were fewer than 100 registered mosques in early 1987 and 300 in 1989, there were said to be 5,000 in mid-1994. Similar developments took place in the other Muslim regions.[20] The large growth in the number of mosques was paralleled by a proportional increase in the number of clergy: in Tatarstan, where there were just 30 clerics at the beginning of the Gorbachev period and 55 mullahs and 12 muezzins in early 1990, there were some 5,000 clerics of various ranks and categories a decade later.[21] Yet in some areas at least, by the late 1990s there was still a serious shortage of properly trained clergy.[22]

---

features, the government providing a single aircraft for the purpose and thus controlling both the number and the identity of the pilgrims. *Islamskii vestnik*, no. 12, 30 June 1992, p. 21.

[18] Bobrovnikov, 'Islam i sovetskoe nasledie v kolkhozakh Severno-Zapadnogo Dagestana', p.134 and 'Islamophobia and Religious Legislation in Daghestan', *Central Asia and the Caucasus*, no. 2, 2000, p. 150. The *hajj* was not undertaken at the expense of visits to local shrines. On page 132 of the former article there is a graphic description of how buses make stops at the various *ziyarats* on their route.

[19] Dmitri Trofimov, 'Friday Mosques and their Imams in the Former Soviet Union', *RSS*, vol. 24, no. 2/3, September 1996, p. 195.

[20] Ibid., p. 217. Another source maintains there were as many as 6,000 mosques in Uzbekistan in 1993. Evgenii Abdullaev, 'Islam i "islamskii faktor" v sovremennom Uzbekistane', *Tsentral'naia Aziia*, no. 6 (12), 1997, p. 87. (It is important to point out that all statistics – for both the Soviet and the post-Soviet periods – have to be taken with a large pinch of salt. This certainly applies to statistics referring to unregistered mosques in the former period. In the mid-1990s it was noted that the Muslim spiritual administrations themselves did not possess precise figures even for the number of Friday mosques in their areas of jurisdiction.)

[21] Mukhametshin, *Islam v obshchestvenno-politicheskoi zhizni Tatarstana*, p. 96.

[22] In Kazakhstan, for example, as of January 1997 just 47 people were studying to be *imam-khatibs* at the Islamic Institute, so that many clergy in the country's 5,000 mosques were still unable to read the Qur'an. Iakov Trofimov, 'Sovremennaia religioznaia situatsiia v Respublike Kazakhstan', p. 63. In Naryn province in Kyrgyzstan, also in 1997, a single mullah served several mosques and 10 villages (*ails*). Georgii Sitnianskii, 'Krest ili polumesiats: Kirgiziia pered vyborom very', *Tsentral'naia Aziia*, no. 6 (12), 1997, p. 79.

The massive expansion of the number of functioning mosques, and especially of officially registered ones, did not signify a corresponding increase in mosque attendance. Observers noted that after a rise in the numbers of worshippers in the Gorbachev period and the first year or so after independence, there was a definite slump, except during the two major festivals. This did not apply everywhere,[23] but it seems to have been a general phenomenon.[24] Thus a sociological survey conducted in the early to mid-1990s disclosed that only 24 per cent of professed believers among Kyrgyz, 18 per cent among Uzbeks and 13 per cent among Kazakhs attended a mosque at least once a month.[25]

The appearance of so many new mosques did not represent only a renascent religious sentiment. In addition to serving as prayer houses, the mosques operated as community centres, reflecting the desire to find new, specifically non-Soviet forms of collective identity. In some areas at least, mosques also acquired property: in northwest Dagestan, for instance, the local administration or leaders of the community, the *jamaat,* restored to mosques a considerable portion of the land (*waqf*), assigned to them prior to collectivization. Once again the income which accrued from it was used to cover the community's religious and social needs.[26] The mosques and their rediscovered social and educational functions (see next section) provided a marked contrast to the recent past, and it became a matter of prestige for a community to acquire this means of signalling a break with the Soviet period.[27] Many mosques became centres for the distribution of religious literature, so sorely lacking during the Soviet era, and people began seeking such literature as soon as the atmosphere became more congenial. Often too the Friday sermon, the *khutba*, became an event of local significance.

Education

The establishment of Muslim educational institutions has been one of the key features of the new Islamic activity. Many of the central figures of the Islamic revival have seen the education and enlightenment of believers on the substance of Islam as

---

[23] In southern Kyrgyzstan, for instance, the numbers of mosque-goers was on the constant increase until the end of the 1990s. Anara Tabyshalieva, 'The Kyrgyz and the Spiritual Dimensions of Daily Life', in Roald Sagdeev and Susan Eisenhower (eds), *Islam and Central Asia: An Enduring Legacy or an Evolving Threat?* (Washington, DC: Center for Political and Strategic Studies, 2000), p. 34.

[24] There may be several reasons for this. It has been suggested, for example, that worshippers might have grown weary of imams concluding the Friday service with prayers for independent Uzbekistan and its leaders. Annette Bohr, *Uzbekistan: Politics and Foreign Policy* (London: RIIA, 1998), p. 28.

[25] Pollock and El Assad (eds), *In the Eye of the Beholder*, pp. 26–7.

[26] Bobrovnikov, 'Islam i sovetskoe nasledie v kolkhozakh Severno-Zapadnogo Dagestana', p. 137.

[27] Shirin Akiner, 'Islam, the State and Ethnicity in Central Asia in Historical Perspective', *RSS*, vol. 24, no. 2/3, September 1996, p. 119.

the basic task of Muslim clerics. According to one leader of the Islamic movement in Uzbekistan during the Gorbachev period, 'education is jihad'.[28] In the words of the Tatarstan mufti Gusman Iskhakov, the Soviet era had led to a loss of understanding of Islam's philosophical, social, economic, moral and legal significance. All strata of the population in the Muslim nationalities therefore had to be re-educated in order to ensure an appropriate comprehension of Islam and the continuation of its spiritual evolution. Mukaddas Bibarsov, the mufti of the Volga Muslim spiritual administration, declared in 1996 that the principal task of the religious community and leadership was to educate the people.[29]

In many cases the clergy themselves were not much better educated in a religious sense than their flock. Throughout most of the 1990s the great majority of rural imams (leaders of prayer) were former unregistered, 'unofficial' mullahs who lacked any religious education and were able to fulfil only elementary religious duties, and even those in a cursory and often canonically erroneous fashion. It was only towards the end of the decade that newly trained cadres began emerging from the relevant institutions of religious studies to take jobs as imams.

Despite the widespread need, Muslim CIS governments were not eager to encourage or even permit religious instruction in the curriculum of public or state educational institutions. This led, in Kyrgyzstan for example, to cases of children leaving the state schools after four or five years and continuing their studies in *madrasas*.[30] Interestingly, a rather large proportion of the Muslim population supports the idea of religious education within the regular school system.[31] At the same time, despite a general awareness that the Soviet regime had substituted first the Latin and then the Cyrillic alphabet for the traditional Arabic one in the educational system in order to cut its Muslim subjects off from their national and religious traditions, there has not been a widespread return to Arabic orthography. In Tajikistan, the only one of the six Muslim successor states whose language law (of 1989) advocated a return to the Arabic script, it was taught in some 200 state schools in the 1991–2 school year, but within two or three years this ceased. By the 2000–01 school year, however, wherever a teacher could be found it had been reintroduced into the school curriculum under the heading 'The heritage of our ancestors'. In Uzbekistan, too, Arabic orthography was taught in some schools for a year or two after the passing of the language law as part of the process of reconnecting to the traditional culture, but this was stopped by

[28] Abdujabar Abduvakhitov, 'Islamic Revivalism in Uzbekistan', in Dale F. Eickelman (ed.), *Russia's Muslim Frontiers: New Directions in Cross-Cultural Analysis* (Bloomington, IN: Indiana University Press, 1993), p. 79.

[29] Mukhametshin, *Islam v obshchestvenno-politicheskoi zhizni Tatarstana*, pp. 111–12.

[30] Dzhumaev, 'Tsentral'naia Aziia: religiia i obshchestvo', p. 13.

[31] According to an opinion research survey in the year 2000, 52 per cent in Azerbaijan, 42 per cent in Kazakhstan and 41 per cent in Uzbekistan favoured this. 'Central Asians Differ on Islam's Political Role', p. 6. The figure for Kazakhstan in 1997 was 53 per cent. Ibid.

the authorities following the outbreak of civil war in neighbouring Tajikistan, as they became concerned at the implications of the re-Islamization of society.[32]

However, schools for religious education – *maktabs* and *madrasas*[33] – did reappear at mosques. These schools, like the renewed charitable functions, were crucial in enabling the mosque to regain something of its traditional influence and status in the local community and to become the arena for grass-roots Islamic activity.[34] According to one source, the new schools in the Fergana Valley had adopted a neo-Hanbali ideology;[35] in other words, they were said to be inculcating Wahhabism in their students. In Kazakhstan as early as 1991 courses were being given at mosques to train the lower rung of clergy, and Sunday schools provided instruction in the Arabic script and the basics of the faith.[36] In Dagestan by the middle of the decade, Arabic and Islamic studies were being taught, mostly by Muslims from abroad, at schools opened at mosques. By mid-1995 there were 650 such schools and groups for teaching young people the basics of the faith, and 25 *madrasas* for the training of religious cadres. Shortly afterwards nine institutes of higher Islamic learning were also reported.[37] The presence of foreign teachers was unavoidable as there were virtually no, or very few, indigenous Muslims who could undertake the teaching of Islam, no textbooks and no financial support from internal sources. As a result, educational institutions were established in an unorganized fashion. In Tatarstan, for instance, the spiritual administration had no coordinating centre which could control or supervise the plethora of new schools.[38]

In addition to local mosque schools, more advanced *madrasas* were opened for higher Islamic training. (Previously, just two such seminaries, in Bukhara and Tashkent, trained clergy for the entire Soviet Union.) By 1994 there were eight such

[32] I am grateful for this information to Muzaffar Olimov of the Sharq Centre in Dushanbe, and to Vladimir Mesamed of the Truman Center, The Hebrew University of Jerusalem.

[33] Strictly speaking, the former were elementary schools and the latter were secondary schools. But in the 1990s this distinction was frequently blurred, and many schools that provided the most elementary religious education called themselves or were commonly called *madrasas*.

[34] The schools, it was noted, shaped the minds and values of children and through them, of their parents. Dmitri Trofimov, 'Friday Mosques and their Imams', p. 194.

[35] Abdullaev, 'Islam i "islamskii faktor"', pp. 88–9. Abdullaev headed the International Department of the National Centre for Human Rights of the Republic of Uzbekistan, and was also a senior lecturer at Tashkent State University. It will be remembered that Wahhabis belong to the Hanbali *madhhab*, whereas in the CIS Sunnis are mostly Hanafis or, in Dagestan, Shafi'is.

[36] A.K. Sultangalieva, 'Islam v Kazakhstane', *Vostok*, 3, 1994, p. 76.

[37] Vladimir Bobrovnikov, 'The Islamic Revival and the National Question in Post-Soviet Dagestan', *RSS*, vol. 24, no. 2/3, 1996, p, 233; Amri Shikhsaidov, 'Islam v Dagestane', *Tsentral'naia Aziia i Kavkaz*, no. 4 (5), 1999, p. 109.

[38] Mukhametshin, *Islam v obshchestvenno-politicheskoi zhizni Tatarstana*, pp. 27–8. This was a cause for concern not only for reasons of prestige but also because sometimes it resulted in teachers from a different Islamic *madhhab* giving instruction to, and therefore probably influencing, local students.

madrasas in Kyrgyzstan, and by 1997 there were seventeen in Bishkek alone.[39] Some of these institutions catered for women students only or conducted courses which accepted women.[40] In Uzbekistan women religious figures, *otyns*, taught in these institutions, although men fulfilled the main teaching and administrative functions.[41]

Here and there 'Islamic universities' were opened. At one of the first to be established in the town of Turkestan in southern Kazakhstan, the teaching personnel all came from abroad. In 1995 another was opened in Kazan. It had five faculties – theology, finance and economics, medicine, law and technology; all studies in the humanities were supposedly based upon Islamic philosophy and practice. In the same year, Islamic universities were inaugurated in Moscow and Baku, the former financed by Kuwait, and the latter, which provided instruction in the Qur'an, the *Hadith* and the *Shari'a* as well as some secular subjects, by Saudi Arabia.[42] However, inevitably, even when these universities were staffed by foreign personnel, their level of teaching could not compare with long-established institutions in other Muslim countries. Many of the so-called Islamic universities and institutes of higher learning were not essentially different from *madrasas*. It was thus inevitable that considerable numbers of students from CIS countries attended Islamic institutions of higher learning in the Arab countries and Turkey. In 1992 several hundred Dagestanis reportedly undertook Islamic studies throughout the Middle East, and by 1996 some 1,500 Dagestani students were enrolled abroad in institutions of Islamic learning.[43]

The status of women and gender relations

The partial reinstatement of Islamic values as the guiding ethic for society that has accompanied the national renascence in post-Soviet Muslim communities has inevitably affected gender relations and the status of women. The traditionalist Islam that is being returned to in Central Asia tends to stress a patriarchal society as part of the revival of Muslim tradition. This involves a major transformation from the sexual egalitarianism that was a central theme of Soviet ideology. According to one source, the erosion of the indicators of female emancipation has been one of the main causes

---

[39] At these establishments, which had been set up under Turkish auspices, students were forbidden even to speak Russian. Sitnianskii, 'Krest ili polumesiats', p. 79. For Turkish activity in the propagation of Islam in Central Asia, see Gareth Winrow, *Turkey in Post-Soviet Central Asia* (London: RIIA, 1995), p. 27.

[40] Kerimov, 'Islam and Muslims in Russia', p. 191; Akiner, 'Islam, the State and Ethnicity', p. 118.

[41] Haiba Fathi, 'Otines: The Unknown Women Clerics of Central Asian Islam', *Central Asian Survey*, vol. 16, no. 1, 1997, p. 40.

[42] Kerimov, 'Islam and Muslims in Russia', p. 191; Lawrence E. Adams, 'The Reemergence of Islam in the South Caucasus', *RSS*, vol. 24, no. 2/3, p. 222; and personal knowledge.

[43] Bobrovnikov, 'The Islamic Revival and the National Question', p. 233; Makarov, *Ofitsial'nyi i neofitsial'nyi islam v Dagestane*, p. 5.

of the large-scale conversion of Kyrgyz and Kazakh women to Protestant Christianity and other faiths that are not traditional to the region.[44]

As some women and girls took up Islamic education at various levels, a few Muslim women's organizations came into being, specifically the League of Muslim Women which surfaced in Kazakhstan, Kyrgyzstan and Uzbekistan. None of them, however, were active for long. At the same time, women have asserted their choice of an Islamic way of life in other, more conventional, ways. Some schoolgirls and university students have begun to wear the *hijab* (headscarf) and ankle- and wrist-length clothes. In parts of the Fergana Valley some older women have returned to the *paranja* (cloak) which covers them from head to toe. But, for the most part, 'the women do not know their rights in Islamic law and are therefore unable to argue their case on those grounds'. Often it is the men who determine their womenfolk's standards of modesty in both dress and behaviour, and who decide whether or not women should be allowed to attend the mosque or play an active role in other religious activities outside the home.[45]

In some parts of the CIS there are women Islamists who hope to play a central role in the re-Islamization of the female population. Many of them have made the pilgrimage to Mecca and have received religious training beyond that of the older generation of *otyns*, enabling them to recite the Qur'an in accordance with established rules of pronunciation and intonation. In Uzbekistan the older *otyns* take courses with these younger women, who define themselves as 'modern and revolutionary *otyns*', and convey their newly acquired skills to their own pupils or adepts within the *mahalla*.[46]

A study on Azerbaijan has stressed that some of the practices seen as Islamic may in fact have been local custom 'preceding or superseding Islam' and that it is difficult to 'maintain the line' between ethnic customs and Islamic ones. It describes the primary sources of national identity in Azerbaijan as ethnicity, language, regionalism and Islam and insists that 'gender discourse' in Azerbaijan's independence movement has not acquired 'a doctrinal or ideologically ("fundamentalist") Islamist tone'. Nevertheless, because the private, domestic domain was the principal 'bastion of resistance' to the regime in the Soviet Muslim east, 'gender roles and intra-family

[44] Tabyshalieva, 'The Kyrgyz and the Spiritual Dimensions of Daily Life', pp. 36–7. For the conversion of Muslims to Christianity in Kyrgyzstan and Kazakhstan, see also Sitnianskii, 'Krest ili polumesiats', pp. 74–5; Sultangalieva, 'Islam v Kazakhstane', pp. 76-8; Trofimov, 'Sovremennaia religioznaia situatsiia v Respublike Kazakhstan', pp. 61 and 63; and *Vremia*, 29 September 2000. There have also been Russians, in Kazakhstan in particular, who have converted to Islam. No statistical data are available about the conversion movement among either Kazakhs or Russians.

[45] Shirin Akiner, 'Between Tradition and Modernity: The Dilemma Facing Contemporary Central Asian Women', in Mary Buckley (ed.), *Post-Soviet Women: from the Baltic to Central Asia* (Cambridge: Cambridge University Press, 1997), p. 286. For the Kazakhstan League of Muslim Women, see Chapter 5 and Sultangalieva, *Islam v Kazakhstane*, pp. 71–2.

[46] Fathi, 'Otines: The Unknown Women Clerics of Central Asian Islam', pp. 40–1.

dynamics have retained strong traditional and religious characteristics', and women were the 'primary carriers of this "religious load"'. Moreover, Azerbaijani women, who with very few exceptions do not wear the veil, take pride in their role as 'maintainers of religion, morality and national heritage'.[47]

Literature

The dearth of Islamic publications, like the scarcity of mosques, trained clergy and educational institutions, was a major problem for believers in the Soviet period. By the late 1970s people were finding ways to bring in literature and even tapes, notably from Khomeini's Iran which was transmitting radio broadcasts to the Muslims of the Soviet Union.[48] Under *glasnost* the Qur'an began to be translated into the languages of the Soviet Union's major Muslim nationalities, and Saudi Arabia undertook to supply large numbers of Qur'ans, first in Arabic and later in Uzbek and Kazakh (see Chapter 7).

Throughout the CIS the supply of Islamic publications and media was an integral part of the Islamic revival. The availability of materials – books, pamphlets, journals, audio and video cassettes and radio and TV broadcasts – and the opportunity to teach and preach Islam openly provided the framework for the revival. This informal education was no less significant than the formal educational establishment as it catered for those who had grown up under communism. Muslim periodicals, namely publications of the spiritual administrations or of other Muslim organizations, did not exist in effect until the 1990s. As late as 1993 only three appear to have existed throughout the Russian Federation – in Moscow (the IRP paper *Vahdat*), in Saratov and in Makhachkala. The chief editor of the third periodical explained that his staff were conducting 'agitation and educational work among the Muslim population, in mosques and *madrasas*, at gatherings and meetings, in the mass media, and so on. In this way [the paper] was promoting the spiritual renascence of the Muslims.' By the end of the decade, however, each major spiritual administration had its own newspaper. So too did a number of Islamic parties, specifically the Russian Union of Muslims (RUM) and the Tatar party Ittifaq.

Most of the Islamic periodical literature did not appear on a regular basis, for lack of funding and competent contributors. Many Islamic journals and newspapers reproduced writings of radical Islamic figures (Khomeini, Maudoodi, Yusuf al-Qirdawi and the leader of the Sudanese Muslim Brothers Hasan at-Turabi). They also carried articles by some of the more important Russian Muslim imams and *ulamas*,

[47] Nayereh Tohidi, 'The Intersection of Gender, Ethnicity and Islam in Soviet and Post-Soviet Azerbaijan', *Nationalities Papers*, vol. 25, no. 1, 1997, pp. 154–5.
[48] See Ro'i, *Islam in the Soviet Union*, pp. 358–9 and 583.

most of whom appeared in the secular press as well – Ravil Gainutdin, Talgat Tajutdin, Mukaddas Bibarsov, Nafigulla Ashirov, Geidar Jemal and Valiahmed Sadur. Perhaps most significant of all, the Islamic press sought to educate its readership in Islam. It reproduced excerpts from the Qur'an with accompanying commentary (*tafsir*) and legends from the life of the Prophet, explained the rules relating to prayer and the significance of the Muslim festivals and devoted space to the history of Islam. Sometimes it even warned against the assimilatory processes Russia's Muslims were undergoing, notably as a result of marriage with non-Muslims, which meant that their children would not read the Qur'an.[49]

In Uzbekistan the regime took upon itself the responsibility to disseminate materials propagating Islamic values and norms – books, journals, television and radio broadcasts – as part of an effort to encourage carefully controlled Islamic activity (see Chapter 6).[50] In Tatarstan a number of publishing houses were subordinate to the official Muslim establishment.[51] The Youth Centre of Islamic Culture had its own paper, *Iman*, as early as 1991, and by 1994 it was also publishing a Russian-language version. In 1993 it had begun publishing Russia's sole academic religious journal, *Islam Nuri*.[52]

Kazakhstan, on the other hand, was still not publishing its own Islamic materials as late as 1997. However, religious books for distribution there, in both Kazakh and Russian, were being published in Turkey and Pakistan while other Islamic literature was being brought in from Russia. The mufti of Kazakhstan, Ratbek Nisanbai-uly, published a Kazakh translation of the Qur'an, in addition to that which was translated in Saudi Arabia. The spiritual administration he headed issued a Muslim newspaper (*Iman*) in Kazakh, Uighur and Chechen, which was later suspended (apparently in 1997), and as of 1997 a monthly journal entitled *Islam Elemi* (World of Islam), with a print run of 5,000.[53]

Summary

The revival of Islam in the CIS has been a complex development which has affected all spheres of life in many of the communities under review. Islam has become markedly more visible, and those aspiring to identify with it actively have been able to find the requisite mentors, institutions of learning and literature. The strength it has been perceived to bestow was manifest in a statement by senior Azerbaijani military

---

[49] Aleksei Malashenko, *Islamskoe vozrozhdenie v sovremennoi Rossii* (Moscow: Carnegie Center, 1998), pp. 88–92.
[50] Abdullaev, 'Islam i "islamskii faktor"', p. 87.
[51] Mukhametshin, *Islam v obshchestvenno-politicheskoi zhizni Tatarstana*, p. 137.
[52] Malashenko, *Islamskoe vozrozhdenie v sovremennoi Rossii*, pp. 88–9.
[53] Iakov Trofimov, 'Sovremennaia religioznaia situatsiia v Respublike Kazakhstan', p. 62.

personnel calling for the introduction of Islamic values into the army to enable it to recover territories lost to Armenia.[54] At the same time, it would be a gross exaggeration to attribute to this renascence far-reaching changes in the lifestyle and world-view of society at large beyond general declarations of identification with Islam. Although, for instance, public debates on introducing Islamic law have become common, *Shari'a* courts have only been established *de facto* in a number of villages in the North Caucasus.[55] On the whole, society in the Muslim regions has remained essentially dormant from the point of view of Islam, being neither prepared to man barricades on its behalf nor even interested in substituting Islamic learning for the prevalent secular curriculum of studies.

[54] The Baku independent *525 Gazet* published on 28 June 2000 a report entitled 'Jihad is the only way to fight against Armenians'. It spoke of a round table held the previous day at the headquarters of the Azerbaijan Karabakh Liberation Movement (AKLM). Its deputy chairman emphasized the need for the army to benefit from the opportunities provided by Islam, given the importance of spiritual and psychological factors in raising combat readiness. The discussion adopted a resolution according to which 'Jihad has always been the moral support of the Azerbaijani people in their struggle against alien invaders. At the current stage, the only way to organize the people's struggle against the Armenian occupiers is to form spiritual values.' To this end, religious propaganda had to be conducted in the army with the help of graduates from Islamic higher schools. I am grateful to Razmik Panossian of the London School of Economics for this information.

[55] Such courts were set up by mosques in Dagestan, Chechnya, Ingushetia, North Ossetia-Alana, Karachaevo-Cherkessia and Kabardino-Balkaria. Vladimir Bobrovnikov, 'Mythologizing Sharia Courts in the Post-Soviet North Caucasus', *ISIM Newsletter*, no. 5, 2000, p. 25. For the introduction of *Shari'a* law in Chechnya, see Chapter 4; for Dagestan, see Chapter 5.

4 THE POLITICIZATION OF ISLAM

Throughout its history Islam has influenced political developments in Muslim societies, for within Islam the differentiation between religion and politics went unrecognized in theory, if not in practice. Islam covered all aspects of social existence and incorporated its own regulating precepts.[1] As all spheres of life fell within its jurisdiction, its theologians and philosophers inevitably dealt with issues that today would be defined as purely political. The division between religion and politics in the Western consciousness created in the sixteenth century and the more general acceptance of that dichotomy since the French Revolution did not affect Muslim communities. It was only the exigencies of industrialization and urbanization and their concomitants that brought a change in this direction, and the twentieth century saw quite a few attempts in the Muslim world to create secular regimes.

The Bukharan Emirate and the khanates of Kokand and Khiva which ruled the sedentary regions of Central Asia were beginning to show signs of relaxing the hold of religion on their everyday affairs prior to the Russian conquest in the second half of the nineteenth century. The Russian empire, for its part, was prepared to tolerate Islam insofar as it agreed to subordinate itself to the state and its requirements (see Chapter 1). The Bolshevik regime was more adamant in its rejection of any avowed public role for religion as a whole and Islam specifically. It did all in its power to abolish completely any possible link between Islam and its own objectives, which were expressed in purely materialistic language. The most it could condone was the practice of religion within registered prayer houses, and this too it sought to restrict in every way. As a result, although Islam persisted as a social regulator in those areas where Muslim nationalities comprised the majority of the population, it departed from the political arena completely. True, Islam's social role continued to have political connotations – certainly in the eyes of the CPSU – and occasionally the regime saw the necessity to repress particularly unwelcome manifestations, but to all intents and purposes it was depoliticized.

Most of the countries which this study surveys have shown signs of at least a partial return to Islam since the disintegration of the Soviet Union, and Islam has once

[1] Cf. Aleksei Malashenko, 'Islam and Politics in Central Asian States', in Jonson and Esenov (eds), *Political Islam and Conflicts in Russia and Central Asia*, p. 11.

again become a political factor in their societies. In the words of the former mufti of Uzbekistan Muhammad Sodyk Mamayusupov, or Muhammad Yusuf, Islam – indeed every religion – has a major political potential which it is impossible to refute.[2] In the year 2000 close to 60 per cent of Muslims in Uzbekistan claimed that Islam played a major role in their country's political life, as did approximately one-third in Tajikistan and Kazakhstan and just under 20 per cent in Azerbaijan.[3]

The perception of the threat

The situation of a basically depoliticized Islam became transformed towards the end of the 1970s. The Islamic Revolution in Iran and the outbreak of civil war in Afghanistan as the *mujahidin* opened their counteroffensive against the Marxist regime which took power there in 1978, changed the attitude of the Soviet leadership to domestic Islam (see Chapter 1). For the first time since the 1920s Moscow appeared apprehensive that events in the Muslim world outside might influence the Soviet political scene. The immediate concern was that the major Muslim nationalities, which had co-nationals in neighbouring countries, might seek to apply lessons learned there to their own situation of subordination to an oppressive regime.

The problem was twofold. In the first place, Islam might prove to be an ideology that would not only undermine the very foundations of Marxism-Leninism, but also consolidate all the country's Muslim nationalities in opposition to Moscow – a resuscitation of the old bogey of pan-Islam. Second, Islam might constitute a slogan that could serve as a cover for other grievances – social, economic and cultural – which the subject nationalities of the Soviet empire would find more difficult to express openly.

It is by no means certain to what extent Andropov, Gorbachev and their colleagues were genuinely fearful regarding the political and security threat immanent in domestic Islam. It does appear that they exploited a phantom threat as a propaganda gimmick in order to legitimize harsher security measures and enhanced repression of what they perceived as Islamic fanaticism. Certainly, the danger seems to have been consciously exaggerated and manipulated by the country's leadership for its own ends. At the same time, the regime's failure in the last years of the Soviet Union to cope with surfacing social and economic issues in the Muslim areas turned them into sources of local political discontent, of which Islam became the mouthpiece. As one analysis has pointed out, a subsistence standard of living, in Tajikistan in particular, meant that the great majority of the population did not enjoy the achievements of modernization. Against this backdrop, Islam appeared to be 'a natural form of expression for the political interests of those social groups who had, as it were, [actually] suffered from

---

[2] Interview with Oleg Panfilov in *Tsentral'naia Aziia*, no. 6 (12), 1997, p. 102.
[3] 'Central Asians Differ on Islam's Political Role', p. 3, Figure 2 and Table 9.

the benefits of progressive change'. Nor, according to this same source, was Islam just a form of, or framework for, political struggle. Given the principle of the inseparability of politics and religion, which had over the centuries made an indelible impression on Islamic civilization, Islam 'puts forward [its own] substantive political reference points and presents [its own] claims'.[4]

Interestingly, the political threat posed by Islam had been transfigured by the mid-1980s. In previous decades Sufism had been considered the central danger to the regime (see Chapter 2). (This perception, like so many others in the Islamic context, had been inherited from tsarist times.) In the 1970s several treatises were published, particularly in the North Caucasus, elaborating on the ways in which Sufism jeopardized the achievements of 'socialist construction'. This applied most notably to the Chechen-Ingush ASSR, where the two eponymous nationalities allegedly made use of the Sufi brotherhoods and their traditions to obstruct the implementation of policy. Sufism was portrayed as a ready-made, historically anti-Russian and anti-Soviet underground network that was awaiting the opportunity to take up arms. By the mid-1980s Sufism was being downplayed: it no longer occupied centre stage. Its place had been taken by a new 'menace' – 'Wahhabism' (see Chapter 2).[5]

First identified publicly in Tajikistan, Wahhabism was said by the Tajikistan Communist Party First Secretary, Qahhor Mahkamov, to be a synthesis of religion and politics that was both nationalist and reactionary.[6] This statement came in the wake of the arrest and trial in Kurgan-Tyube of an unregistered itinerant mullah, Abdullo Saidov, who was said to be an adherent of Wahhabism and to have called for the establishment of an Islamic state in Tajikistan and for the use of arms to achieve this.[7]

It is uncertain whether Saidov was in fact a Wahhabi. The same doubt holds for others in Tajikistan and the Fergana Valley similarly labelled Wahhabis in the last years of Soviet rule[8] and following independence, most of whom denied any affiliation

[4] Aleksei Malashenko and Vladimir Moskalenko, 'Proigralo li religioznoe dvizhenie v Tadzhikistane?', *Nezavisimaia gazeta*, 31 January 1992.

[5] One of the first scholars to draw attention to the substitution of Wahhabism for Sufism was Muriel Atkin. See her chapter 'Islam as Faith, Politics and Bogeyman in Tajikistan', in Michael Bourdeaux (ed.), *The Politics of Religion in Russia and the New States of Eurasia* (Armonk, NY, and London: M.E. Sharpe, 1995), pp. 251–3.

[6] *Kommunist Tadzhikistana*, 3 September 1986.

[7] *Kommunist Tadzhikistana*, 31 January and 12 and 28 February 1987. It has been suggested that the term 'Wahhabism' was already in use in informal contexts before 1986, but it is not clear exactly where or when its application to certain people or trends in the Fergana Valley and Tajikistan originated. Some contend that it was first employed by the KGB, others that it was introduced by Moscow-based Arabists, and a third view believes it to have been applied by the Central Asian Muslim establishment in its efforts to calumniate the central figures of popular Islam.

[8] One Uzbek scholar who has discussed this development prefers to call the Fergana Valley's Islamic reformers Proto-Wahhabis. Babadzhanov, 'The Fergana Valley: Source or Victim of Islamic Fundamentalism?', pp. 112–16. See also Chapter 3.

with Wahhabism. It would probably have been far more appropriate to classify them as Salafis – people seeking to restore Islam to its pristine precepts, norms and values – which is what they called themselves.

Of far greater significance than the actual association of Central Asian Islamic activists with Wahhabism was the way the regime portrayed Wahhabism in the domestic arena and the fact that this became the context for condemning anti-establishment Islamic figures. Characterized as extremists, fundamentalists and sectarians – strictly speaking, there was more justification for calling Wahhabis, rather than Sufis, sectarians – they were placed beyond the pale. Wahhabism had the additional advantage, from the point of view of regime propaganda, of being linked with Saudi Arabia, where the sect had originated in the eighteenth century and where it persisted in the twentieth century as official doctrine (see Chapter 3). This automatically made its adherents agents of a foreign and, in the Soviet period, hostile state. A Soviet commentator who served as a regime mouthpiece on the issue of the Islamic threat to Moscow indeed linked the Afghanistan government-in-exile, which he described as Wahhabi-dominated and backed by the United States and Saudi Arabia, to the spread of Wahhabism in Soviet Central Asia.[9]

The term 'Wahhabism' remains in use to denigrate Islamists in both Central Asia and the North Caucasus in the post-Soviet period, although the basic characteristics of Islamist movements there are social activism and non-conformism rather than adherence to any specific Islamic doctrine. In most cases, then, the term is applied with no greater legitimacy than under the Soviet regime, except in Dagestan, where there is a genuine link with Wahhabism and where the movement has penetrated and taken root in a number of rural areas.[10] However, even in the North Caucasus – in Dagestan, Chechnya and Ingushetia (two further republics where Wahhabism has surfaced) – Wahhabis prefer to call themselves Salafis.[11] The basic feature of their 'fundamentalist' ideology comprises, on the one hand, a rejection of changes that have occurred within Islam over the centuries, such as the worship of holy shrines (which has brought them into conflict with the Sufi orders), and, on the other hand, a refutation of external, basically Western, influences. Whatever the justification for using the term 'Wahhabi', clearly many of the Islamists so designated have a strong sense of mission to diverge from the social and political conformism of the Muslim establishment, thus exposing themselves to regime repression. At the same time, the Wahhabis, or Salafis, did not comprise a homogeneous group.[12]

[9] *Literaturnaia gazeta*, 13 September 1989.

[10] See Galina M. Yemelianova, 'Islam and Nation Building in Tatarstan and Dagestan of the Russian Federation', *Nationalities Papers*, vol. 27, no. 4, 1999, pp. 620–1.

[11] Vakhit Akaev, 'Religiozno-politicheskii konflikt v Chechenskoi Respublike Ichkeriia', *Tsentral'naia Aziia i Kavkaz* 4 (5), 1999, p. 100.

[12] For their divisions in Dagestan, see Chapter 5. Makarov, *Ofitsial'nyi i neofitsial'nyi islam v Dagestane*, pp. 31–2.

Islamic movements and parties

As of 1989, with the new opportunities provided by *perestroika* and *glasnost*, religious activists in many Muslim regions began to organize movements and parties with the aim of strengthening Islamic influence on both politics and everyday life. For the most part these Islamic political associations were decried by the official Muslim establishment, including figures such as Mamayusupov, who were not averse to Islam playing a political role. The formal position of these critics was that Islam was an entity unto itself whose strength was in its unity, and any fraction within it merely led to its fragmentation and therefore weakened it.[13] Islamic slogans and banners and pictures of Khomeini were noted at many of the disturbances which occurred in Central Asia and Azerbaijan in 1989 and 1990. At demonstrations in Dushanbe in February 1990, as had happened a year earlier in Buinaksk (see Chapter 2), people even shouted 'Long live the Islamic Republic of Tajikistan'.[14] Although this most extreme goal of political Islam, the establishment of an Islamic state, remained no more than a rallying cry, it featured in the platforms of some of the Islamic political parties.[15]

The most important Islamic party prior to the break-up of the Soviet Union was the All-Union Islamic Revival Party (see Chapter 2). It was founded in June 1990 and boasted a membership of some 15,000 from most of the ethnically Muslim union and autonomous republics, Moscow and other regions of the RSFSR with significant Muslim populations.[16] The party set up its permanent headquarters in Moscow in order to be at the centre of the country's political life. Despite an impressive start, the IRP never registered in the Russian Federation after independence. In April 1992 it underwent an undeclared split, the more moderate group organizing a regional conference in Saratov of the Muslims of the European part of Russia and Siberia. In the following year the leader of this wing sought to reorganize the party on a new basis, affirming that it would operate within guidelines provided by the Russian constitution. The party took on an increasingly Tatar orientation, however, and although

---

[13] For Mamayusupov's position on this issue, see Abduvakhitov, 'Islamic Revivalism in Uzbekistan', p. 87; for that of his counterpart, Akbar Turajonzoda, see below. For the opposition of Talgat Tajutdin and Ravil Gainutdin in the mid-1990s to the establishment of Islamic parties in Russia, see Malashenko, *Islamskoe vozrozhdenie*, pp. 139 and 145.

[14] See Y. Ro'i, 'The Islamic Influence on Nationalism in Soviet Central Asia', *Problems of Communism*, vol. 39, no. 4, July–August 1990, pp. 59–64, and 'Central Asian Riots and Disturbances, 1989–1990: Causes and Context', *Central Asian Survey*, vol. 10, no. 3, 1991, pp. 29 and 36.

[15] For further details, see below.

[16] It should be noted that the reliability of statistics regarding party membership, probably of all parties in the Gorbachev period and in the Soviet Union's successor states and certainly of Muslim ones, is open to doubt.

28

it tried to demonstrate that it was functioning within a 'common Islamic space', its activity as a country- or CIS-wide political party petered out.[17]

The All-Union IRP bred a number of republican parties of the same name. The most important of these was unquestionably the IRP of Tajikistan (IRPT). Allowed to register in late 1991, it was the only organization connected with the IRP ever to be officially registered. It became the focus of the opposition that challenged the communist or para-communist hardline regime in a series of large-scale demonstrations in spring 1992 and joined the coalition government which ruled the country from May to September of that year. After the party was outlawed in June 1993, its leaders took refuge abroad, mostly in Afghanistan, where they succeeded in organizing an armed opposition, the United Tajik Opposition (UTO). Its head, Said Abdullo Nuri, was the Abdullo Saidov who had been arrested and accused of Wahhabism in 1986 (see above). (At this point the IRPT became the Islamic Revival Movement.) In the wake of the 1997 settlement of the Tajik civil war and the agreement allotting 30 per cent of posts in the government and administration to the opposition, the IRM leadership returned to Tajikistan's political arena, and in autumn 1999 the IRPT was re-registered as a political party. It won 7.5 per cent of the votes in the parliamentary elections in February 2000 – after the withdrawal from its leadership of Akbar Turajonzoda, First Deputy Chairman and former Qazi Kalon (or Supreme Qazi, the leading figure in the country's Muslim establishment). Dissociating himself publicly from the IRPT, he denounced as erroneous both factually and from the point of view of the *Shari'a* its claims truly to represent Islam. Turajonzoda returned to his previous position, according to which no political party could objectively identify with Islam, as every political party was by definition divisive rather than universal. Far from promoting Islam's development, he contended, the IRPT had hindered this process. Moreover, he accused it of splitting the clergy and the country's Muslim community.[18] The IRPT had forfeited its popularity and the support of the population except in Karategin.

A republican IRP was also formed in Dagestan and in Chechnya in 1990 – as affiliates of the All-Union IRP. Both the Dagestan IRP and the Islamiyya party, which was ideologically close to the Muslim Brotherhood (the most widespread organized Islamic movement in the Middle East), advocated the gradual Islamization of society and the transformation of Dagestan into an Islamic state independent of the Russian

[17] For the IRP, see Sadur, '"Islamskii faktor"', pp. 224–36, and Alexei Malashenko, 'Does Islamic Fundamentalism Exist in Russia?', in Yaacov Ro'i (ed.), *Muslim Eurasia: Conflicting Legacies* (London: Frank Cass, 1995), pp. 43–5.

[18] *Narodnaia gazeta*, 25 February 2000. On the IRPT in earlier years, see Grigorii G. Kosach, 'Tajikistan: Political Parties in an Inchoate Space', in Ro'i (ed.), *Muslim Eurasia*, pp. 123–42, passim. See also Vladimir Babak, Demian Vaisman and Arye Vasserman (eds), *Political Organization in Central Asia and Azerbaijan: Sources and Documents* (London: Frank Cass, forthcoming).

Federation. Neither party, however, enjoyed significant success among the population. They reached the peak of their political activity in 1993, and by the following year they were being consistently isolated by the republican authorities.[19]

In addition to the IRP, a number of other Islamic parties surfaced both in the Russian Federation and in the Muslim states of the CIS. The regions affected in the former included the North Caucasus, particularly Dagestan, and Tatarstan. In Dagestan the Islamic Democratic Party was set up in 1990 by democratically oriented Dagestani intellectuals. Its original programme presented a combination of Islamic and democratic objectives and ideals and was virulently opposed to the ruling *nomenklatura*. In 1994 the party split into two. The activity of the group which retained the old platform petered out while the other faction agreed to cooperate with the ruling regime and became the Islamic Party of Dagestan. Its leaders were co-opted as members of state bodies responsible for Islamic affairs. They advocated integrating *Shari'a* law into the Dagestani legal system, substituting Friday for Sunday as the statutory day of rest, creating an Islamic educational system, including the establishment of an Islamic university, and increasing the number of Islamic radio and television programmes. There have also been Dagestani branches of the Russian Union of Muslims, whose leader was elected Dagestani deputy to the Russian State Duma in 1996, and of the popular political movement Nur.[20]

In Tatarstan the various nationalist organizations, movements and parties adopted an increasingly Islamic orientation during the 1990s. At its fourth conference in December 1997, the radical nationalist party, Ittifaq, declared the national liberation movement being conducted against the Russian empire a *jihad*. It also stated on the same occasion: 'We Muslim nationalists are initiating a struggle for the creation of an Islamic state in Tatarstan.'[21] The clergy itself made several attempts to create some sort of political organization. The most notable of these was Muslims of Tatarstan, formed in June 1996 with the avowed goal of creating an Islamic faction in the Tatarstan parliament. Headed by the mufti of Tatarstan, Gabdulla Galiullin, it was a regional affiliate of the all-Russia socio-political movement Muslims of Russia (see below).[22] Representatives of non-official Islam also formed a number of Islamic groups. Altogether, however, nothing very much came of any of these, and they attracted only small numbers of followers.[23]

[19] Yemelianova, 'Islam and Nation Building in Tatarstan and Dagestan', p. 616. For the Islamiyya, see also Makarov, *Ofitsial'nyi i neofitsial'nyi islam v Dagestane*, pp. 32–3.

[20] Ibid., pp. 613 and 616–17. For details concerning RUM and Nur (later to become the Party of Russian Muslims, PRM), see below.

[21] Mukhametshin, *Islam v obshchestvenno-politicheskoi zhizni Tatarstana*, p. 74.

[22] Malashenko, *Islamskoe vozrozhdenie v sovremennoi Rossii*, p. 149.

[23] Yemelianova, 'Islam and Nation Building in Tatarstan and Dagestan', p. 615. For Muslims of Tatarstan, see Mukhametshin, *Islam v obshchestvenno-politicheskoi zhizni Tatarstana*, pp. 82–5.

In Uzbekistan the IRP was never allowed to register, and its leadership was persecuted and arrested.[24] Perhaps in the absence of an umbrella organization, a number of alternative frameworks came into being. The first of these, chronologically, seems to have been Islom Lashkari, the Warriors of Islam – as a section of the Qurbashi or Basmachi had designated themselves in the 1920s – which appeared in Namangan before the final break-up of the Soviet Union. One of its associated groups, Adolat (Justice), was formed in 1991 with the approval of the *oblast* (regional) authorities in order to act as an autonomous militia for the enforcement of basic Islamic values and *Shari'a* norms and for the prevention of crime. Adolat squads were created in parts of Namangan Oblast and in other regions of the Fergana Valley, notably in Kokand. Replacing the regular agencies for maintaining law and order, they patrolled the streets and bazaars, detained persons suspected of engaging in un-Islamic behaviour and then tried them in ad hoc courts. Adolat's membership was approximately 12,000, and it enjoyed considerable support as a vigilante response to petty crime and official corruption. In this context President Karimov went to Namangan to address a 40,000-strong demonstration staged by Adolat and other affiliated groups on the eve of the presidential election.[25] The demands presented to him included the declaration of Islam as Uzbekistan's state religion and ideology, the introduction of the *Shari'a*, and the legalization of opposition publications. Three months later, when he felt more entrenched in power, President Karimov arrested Adolat activists, and shortly afterwards the group was forced to cease all activity.[26]

Likewise linked to Islom Lashkari were groups of so-called Wahhabis who focused on the discussion of religious questions. Altogether there were said to be some sixty such groups, of twenty to fifty members each. Their leader was Tohir Yoldosh, and they may have operated under the auspices of the Islamic Centre, which Yoldosh and Jumabai Khojiev, more commonly known as Juma Namangani, were later accused of having initiated in Namangan in October 1991.[27]

Another organization was Tawba (Penitence) or Hizb-Allah (Party of God), which had a membership of 300, came into existence, according to different sources, in

---

[24] For details, see Interview of Muhammad Sodyk Muhammad Yusuf with Oleg Panfilov in *Tsentral'-naia Aziia*, no. 6 (12), 1997, pp. 104–5.

[25] At this time, Karimov was no longer party secretary, and was already president, although not by election; he was now standing for presidency in elections.

[26] Vitalii Ponomarev, 'Islam v Uzbekistane, 1989–1995', *Polis*, no. 2, 1996, p. 186; Abdullaev, 'Islam i "islamskii faktor" v sovremennom Uzbekistane', p. 89; William Fierman, 'Political development in Uzbekistan: democratization?', in Karen Dawisha and Bruce Parrott (eds), *Conflict, Cleavage and Change in Central Asia and the Caucasus*, p. 382; and Abdumanob Polat, 'The Islamic Revival in Uzbekistan: A Threat to Stability?', in Sagdeev and Eisenhower (eds), *Islam and Central Asia*, pp. 45–6. According to Polat, 27 Adolat activists were arrested; according to Ponomarev, 'about 100'.

[27] Sentence passed by the Supreme Court of the Republic of Uzbekistan, 17 November 2000, *Pravda vostoka*, 23 November 2000.

either 1990 or 1992, and survived until 1995. Its declared goals included restoring the norms of the *Shari'a* and strengthening the nation's moral foundations.[28]

More significant was Hizb al-Tahrir al-Islami (literally the Islamic Liberation Party). Originally formed in Jerusalem (Jordan) in 1953 following a split in the Muslim Brotherhood, the principal goal of Hizb al-Tahrir was to establish a single Islamic state or caliphate with the help of ideological work consisting of general instruction and political education. Its members are generally committed to participating in *jihad* and it is characterized by underground activity and secretiveness. Its organization is cellular, on the assumption that small groups must be trained as a first stage to training the masses. An international movement, it had branches in the United Kingdom, Jordan and Pakistan, linked through the generation, translation and distribution of literature. In Central Asia, where its first cells appeared in Kokand in 1992–3, Hizb al-Tahrir operated in strict secrecy in small groups of three to ten people. Among other activities, they translated into the local languages the books of the party's founders, which expounded its main ideas and objectives, and the methods by which these were to be attained, and described the future state system. Indeed, Hizb al-Tahrir's activity in Uzbekistan was primarily propagandistic. It insisted that its activity was confined solely to the realm of instructing and convincing believers, but the authorities in both Uzbekistan and Tajikistan were adamant that it included resorting to taking up arms whenever this might be deemed expedient or necessary.[29] It has been suggested by a Western source that the crackdown and mass arrests of 1998 led Hizb al-Tahrir leaders to move from advocating solely peaceful means for achieving their goals to contending that the only effective way to oppose the Karimov regime was through violence.[30]

There seems to be no way of measuring the extent of support for Hizb al-Tahrir. However, it was probably considerable in both Uzbekistan and Tajikistan by the end of the 1990s, given, on the one hand, the mounting dissatisfaction with the harsh regimes of Presidents Karimov and Rahmonov and, on the other hand, the impracticability of a return to former Islamic models and institutions. In Uzbekistan these structures had been repressed (their members being arrested or exiled) and in Tajikistan they had failed to adapt to the new conditions and became discredited (see above).

---

[28] Ashirbek Muminov, 'Traditional and Modern Religious-Theological Schools in Central Asia', in Jonson and Esenov (eds), *Political Islam and Conflicts in Russia and Central Asia*, pp. 109–10, and Aleksandr Khalmuhamedov, 'Islamskii faktor v Uzbekistane', *Svobodnaia mysl'*, no. 4, 1998, p. 55. According to Khalmuhamedov, Hizb-Allah and Tawba were two separate organizations. A party named Tawba operated in Pakistan and Bangladesh, and there may well have been a connection between the two parties.

[29] Muminov, 'Traditional and Modern Religious–Theological Schools in Central Asia', p. 110; document of Hizb al-Tahrir, 20 April 1999, Internet; *Narodnaia gazeta*, 22 June 2000.

[30] *Central Asia: Islamist Mobilisation and Regional Security*, ICG Report No. 14, Osh/Brussels, 1 March 2001.

Interestingly, in the latter country the main area of Hizb al-Tahrir activity appears to be the Leninabad (now Sugd) region in the north, where 39 of the 47 activists arrested in summer 1999 resided. Altogether, by summer 2000 over 100 party activists had been arrested and, according to Tajikistan's interior minister, leaflets and other printed literature calling for the overthrow of the existing system and a fight against infidels had been seized. A large number of the party's followers in Tajikistan were said to be Uzbek nationals from the Uzbek part of the Fergana Valley.[31] According to one source, Hizb al-Tahrir also produced splinter groups, which sought to adapt its methods and tactics to local, Central Asian conditions. One group, founded by Akram Yoldosh in Andijan in 1995 or 1996, was known as Akramiyya (or Khalifatchilar); its activity was banned and its founder arrested.[32]

Hizb al-Tahrir and other movements and groups, including Akramiyya, surfaced in the mid- and late 1990s in southern Kyrgyzstan as well. By the year 2000 it was becoming common to see Hizb al-Tahrir leaflets on house walls and bus-stops in Osh and Jalalabad districts calling on Muslims to return to an Islamic lifestyle.[33] According to the Kyrgyz Ministry of Internal Affairs in 2000, approximately 200 Hizb al-Tahrir emissaries had been detained over the past two years and large numbers of leaflets and much literature calling for *jihad* and the overthrow of the Central Asian governments had been confiscated.[34] Hizb al-Tahrir was also reported to be 'stepping up' its recruitment efforts in southern Kazakhstan in late 2000.[35] In fact, Hizb al-Tahrir leaflets were appearing under doors of people all across Central Asia on a regular basis.[36]

Another political movement surfaced in 1996, the Islamic Movement of Uzbekistan (IMU), headed by Tohir Yoldosh with Juma Namangani as its military commander. In 1992, in the wake of Karimov's repressions both men took refuge in Tajikistan, where they linked up with the United Tajik Opposition (UTO). When the IRPT leadership fled that country Yoldosh and Namangani and their adherents accompanied them and underwent military training in Afghanistan. Before returning to Tajikistan with the UTO, they seem also to have spent periods of time in Pakistan, Iran and Turkey. Over the years Karimov's repression of Islamic 'extremism' brought large numbers of refugees to Tajikistan, where many joined Namangani's force. According to what are considered to be credible reports, their force comprised 50–100 members between 1992 and 1995, but its ranks were swelled by subsequent persecution in Uzbekistan.

---

[31] *Narodnaia gazeta*, 22 June 2000, and ITAR-TASS, 25 August 2000. I am indebted to Dmitrii Makarov of the Moscow Institute of Oriental Studies for information on Hizb al-Tahrir.

[32] Babadzhanov, 'The Fergana Valley: Source or Victim of Islamic Fundamentalism?', pp. 129–30.

[33] *Nezavisimaia gazeta*, 12 April 2001.

[34] The *Uzbekistan Report*, 17 December 2000, *www.uzreport.com*, quoting the Kyrgyz *Liberal'naia gazeta* website, 30 November 2000. For the nature and extent of Hizb al-Tahrir activity in Kyrgyzstan, see also *Nezavisimaia gazeta*, 12 April 2001.

[35] *The Uzbekistan Report*, 2 January 2001.

[36] *Central Asia: Islamist Mobilisation and Regional Security*, pp. 19–20.

By early 1998 Tashkent was speaking of 1,000 Uzbek *mujahidin* and two years later Afghan sources spoke of 2,000 IMU fighters in Afghanistan (see below). It has been emphasized by a number of commentators, both Uzbek and Western, that although the IMU has had links with the Taliban and may well be receiving financial and other assistance from similar, even the same, sources, the mainspring of its support has been from inside Uzbekistan. In May 2001 Namangani reportedly created in Afghanistan a new party, the Hezb-e-Islami of Turkestan, which set itself the aim of Islamizing Central Asia, including China's Xinjiang Uyghur Autonomous Region.[37]

One further party deserving of attention is the Islamic Party of Azerbaijan (IPA), founded in 1991 and officially registered the following year. The party's ideology contended that Islam alone could play a constructive role in the creation of an independent Azerbaijan, and that in order for the country to resolve the crisis situation in which it found itself its leadership needed to adopt Islamic values and Islamic notions of state-building. The IPA's propaganda attacked nationalism and the concept of Pan-Turkism, which it feared was intended as a substitute for the Muslim *umma*. The West too was a major enemy and particularly the international Masonic conspiracy with its centre in Israel. By the end of 1994 the party had branches in more than 70 districts and towns and a membership of some 50,000. It also began training Islamic brigades. This activity, however, brought down the wrath of the authorities, and in 1995 the party's application to re-register was turned down. Its activities were said to be hostile to the interests of the state, its leaders were arrested and in 1997 charges were brought against them. They were accused of spying for Iran and attempting a *coup d'état*, and received ten-year sentences of imprisonment.[38] Although apparently not formally reinstated, the party has continued to function, even nominating a candidate to the parliamentary elections in 2000.[39]

Islam and secular parties and movements

Islamic themes surfaced in the programmes of secular movements. This applied in particular to nationalist movements as well as strictly Islamic formations, which identified Islam with the ethnic culture or saw it as one of its essential ingredients.[40]

[37] Polat, 'The Islamic Revival in Uzbekistan: A Threat to Stability?', pp. 46–7; ICG, *Central Asia Briefing*, 18 October 2000, p. 8; sentence passed by the Supreme Court of the Republic of Uzbekistan, 17 November 2000; *The Times of Central Asia* on the web (*www.times.kg*); and RFE/RL, 6 June 2001.

[38] Igor Rotar, 'Islamic Fundamentalism in Azerbaijan: Myth or Reality?', *Prism*, vol. 6, August 2000. See also Babak, Vaisman and Vasserman (eds), *Political Organization in Central Asia and Azerbaijan*.

[39] Interfax, 4 October 2000. I am indebted for this information to Hratch Tchilingirian of the London School of Economics.

[40] The reasons for this were sundry and are extraneous to this study. Suffice it to say here that sometimes this view was a reflection of innate perceptions of nationalist intelligentsias, sometimes a consequence of tactical considerations and sometimes a reaction to or imitation of the connection made between Russian nationalism and Russian Orthodoxy (see Chapter 2).

The most blatant example of the use of Islam by movements and parties that were basically secular involved the two all-Russian Muslim organizations, the Russian Union of Muslims and Nur, which in 1998 became the Party of Russian Muslims (PRM). Both were created in 1995 with the intention of representing the interests of the ethnic Muslim nationalities of the Russian Federation in the forthcoming parliamentary elections. RUM's leaders said at its founding convention that their aim was to unite the country's Muslims and represent their interests 'in all the branches and structures of government'.[41] (A third movement, the Islamic Committee, came into being in the context of the elections under the slogan of union with Russian Orthodox Christianity to withstand the West, but it soon petered out.) RUM and Nur both addressed themselves at least formally to the spiritual aspect of Islam and opposed 'nationalism and religious extremism'. The former stated that it sought to 'take into account the specific traditions, cultural heritage and basic precepts of Islam'. Claiming to be the heir of the organization of the same name that had participated in the elections to the first Russian Duma after the 1905 revolution, RUM affiliated itself to the Russian Prime Minister Viktor Chernomyrdin's party, Russia – Our Home. Nur, on the other hand, stood independently, including in its programme 'the revival and consolidation of Muslim traditions [and] the Muslim way of life'. It also hoped to obtain state subsidies for Muslim schools and other foundations and institutions and advocated the formation of Muslim divisions in Russia's armed forces. Although no fewer than 72 branches were opened throughout the country, in the elections it polled fewer than 400,000 votes, representing less than one-tenth of Russia's Muslim voters – although in Ingushetia it received 24 per cent of the votes and in Chechnya 18 per cent – and it did not win any seats in the State Duma.[42]

In the course of the 1990s further attempts were made to unite the country's Muslims on a political basis. The first of these took place in Saratov in April 1996, prior to the presidential elections, when the Muslims of Russia came into being as a 'socio-political movement'. Its leader, Mukaddas Bibarsov, stated that the only reason he entertained doubts regarding support for Yeltsin was the war in Chechnya, where 'our Muslim brethren' were being killed. The movement's political council included Valiahmed Sadur, one of the founders of the All-Union IRP, and Talib Saidbaev, editor of the journal of the Moscow muftiate.[43] The second initiative occurred in early 1999, under the name of the All-Russia Islamic Congress.[44]

[41] *Segodnia*, 2 September 1995.
[42] Erik Komarov, 'The Elections in Russia and the Muslims', *Rossiia i musul'manskii mir*, no. 5 (47), 1996, pp. 24–9, and Shikhsaidov, 'Islam v Dagestane', p. 111. For the evolution of RUM and Nur and their role in Russian politics, see also Malashenko, *Islamskoe vozrozhdenie v sovremennoi Rossii*, pp. 136–48.
[43] *Izvestiia*, 16 April 1996; Malashenko, *Islamskoe vozrozhdenie v sovremennoi Rossii*, pp. 142–3.
[44] Shikhsaidov, 'Islam v Dagestane', p. 111.

In some of the Muslim successor states, secular political parties sought to include Islamic motifs in their political programmes for the crystallization of a secular state. Among these parties were Musavat in Azerbaijan, Alash in Kazakhstan and Asaba in Kyrgyzstan. Although they were principally nationalist movements with nationalist programmes, they nonetheless felt that they could not truly represent their respective national cultures without addressing themselves to the Islamic component of these cultures and making demands to improve the lot of Islam in their respective countries. As one of Alash's co-chairmen pointed out in an interview, the crescent moon, the symbol of Islam, adorned the front page of the party newspaper, and being a Muslim and praying in the mosque, 'if not every day, at least as often as possible', were preconditions for joining the party.[45]

An Islamic state? The case of Chechnya

In Chechnya there was unquestionably an element of political strategy in the Islamic emphasis given to his programme by Johar Dudayev, the former Soviet air force general who headed the Chechen Republic from late 1991 until his death in 1996. It is important to stress this in any attempt to assess how far Chechnya could be perceived as an Islamic state.

It should be kept in mind that religious figures had stood at the forefront of Chechen opposition to Moscow for decades (see Chapter 1), and even to St Petersburg in the eighteenth and nineteenth centuries. As one source pointed out, the fact that the struggle for political independence had been conducted historically under the flag of establishing an independent Islamic state made it perfectly natural in the 1990s for Chechnya's separatist opposition to the federal centre to join battle using Islamic slogans.[46] Between December 1990 and February 1991 the Vainakh Democratic Party (VDP)[47] and Islamic activists organized a series of demonstrations under the slogan of Muslim solidarity. According to one scholar, massive pro-Iraqi demonstrations in the context of the Gulf War, conducted under this slogan, helped radical Chechen nationalists win popular backing, and the head of the committee which coordinated pro-Iraqi activity in the republic actually attempted to create a Party for the Defence

---

[45] *Kazakhstanskaia pravda*, 14 November 1990, and see Babak, Vaisman and Vasserman (eds), *Political Organization in Central Asia and Kazakhstan.* Alash's activity petered out in 1993. When it re-entered the political arena in 1999, its programme, emphases and slogans were different and there seemed no longer to be any reference to Islam. S.A. D'ianenko, L.I. Karmazina and S.T. Seidumanov, *Politicheskie partii Kazakhstana 2000 god* (Almaty, 2000), pp. 29–38.

[46] M.S. Ashimbaev and A. Zh. Shomanov, 'Politizatsiia islama na postsovetskom prostranstve: uroki i vyzovy dlia Kazakhstana', *Analytic – Analiticheskoe obozrenie*, 1 October 2000, p. 11.

[47] Vainakh was the common name for the Chechen and Ingush.

36

of Islam.[48] These radical nationalists also received the support of Dudayev when he demobilized and became the *de facto* leader of the National Congress Executive Committee in 1991. And when Dudayev attacked the Russian 'colonial empire' at the second session of the Chechen National Congress in June 1991, he contended that it had deprived the Chechen people of their values and treasures, among which he enumerated Islam as the first. Dudayev stressed that the CPSU and the KGB had conducted a campaign against Islam as the sole force capable of uniting the Caucasian peoples in their resistance to foreign ideologies and beliefs.

In the wake of the failed August 1991 putsch this politicization of Islam realized its potential. The Islamists stood at the head of demonstrations directed against the apparatchiks who had been compromised by their support of the coup attempt, and the VDP Executive Committee assigned the task of creating its strike force or national guard to the leader of the Islamic Path Party (Islaman Neq) which had come into being the previous year. Volunteers for this force mobilized under the slogan of a *ghazavat* or holy war (the Caucasian version of *jihad*). The autumn of 1991 also saw the division of the Chechen-Ingush ASSR into two separate republics, the one Chechen, the other Ingush, and the election of Dudayev as Chechen president.

As the situation between Moscow and Grozny deteriorated following Dudayev's declaration of Chechen independence and Yeltsin's countermeasures, Dudayev did not hesitate to play the Islamic card. In subsequent months it seemed that Chechnya was not merely shaping up as an Islamic state, but that it might become a magnet for non-Chechen North Caucasian Muslims. However, neither Dudayev nor the VDP leadership, the ideologues of the 'Chechen revolution', declared themselves in favour of an Islamic state, and the constitution passed by parliament in March 1992 simply declared Chechnya a state governed by democratic law, making no mention of Islam as either a majority or a national religion.

Yet, while insisting that he preferred a constitutional, secular state, Dudayev stressed that the colonial power had singled out Islam as the sole force capable of uniting the Caucasian peoples in their resistance to foreign ideologies, and therefore Islam required special attention in the 'new power structure'. Furthermore, although Islamic law did not enjoy formal status, officials had to take their oath of office on the Qur'an and the parliament decreed that in conformity with Islamic law and morals autopsies were not to be conducted except in special cases, and men were not to serve as gynaecologists. Yet another indication of tacit Islamicization was the leading role played by the Chechen tribal *aksakals* (elders) in the Chechen revolution, in particular by the Mehk Kel, the traditional Chechen Council of Elders, set up in December 1991

---

[48] This statement and, indeed, most of the section on Chechnya have been taken from Alexis Koudriavtsev, 'L'imamat du General Doudaev ou l'islam et la politique en Tchetchénie', *MANA, Revue de sociologie et d'anthropologie, religion et politique*, Caen: Université de Caen, 1996, pp. 63–89.

and composed of some of the more extreme *aksakals*. As early as February 1992 the Mehk Kel declared that Islam was to be considered Chechnya's dominant faith. Two months later Dudayev installed a National Committee for the Affairs of the Muslim Faith; its specific task was to promote Islam's revival within the country and to coordinate and consolidate ties with foreign Muslim organizations. Several weeks earlier Dudayev had denounced an attempted coup by the local opposition as having violated Islamic norms.

As relations between Dudayev and the parliament worsened, the Islamists gained ground. The general social and economic crisis in which the country found itself naturally paved the way for authoritarian and populist rule – at the expense of democracy and 'modernism' – and in the context of Chechnya, populism presupposed Islamic values and symbols. Dudayev's supporters had declared him imam of Chechnya as early as April 1992, a position that indisputably helped him to disarm the opposition. In July 1992 the Mehk Kel and other Muslim institutions recommended to the president that he dissolve parliament. They also sought to reinforce the status of the *Shari'a*, an initiative which Dudayev supported in early 1993 as his political situation seemed jeopardized. In October 1992 he had told a Russian journalist that he would be happy to be able to declare Chechnya an Islamic state; in February 1993 he proposed amendments to the constitution, according to which Islam was to be the state religion and Islamic courts were to be established alongside civil ones. In April 1993, as opposition to his rule mounted, Dudayev, although carefully avoiding any mention of his role as imam, persisted in presenting himself as the true defender of Islam, and his rivals as its enemies and infidels. His most enthusiastic supporters were villagers, *murids* or adepts of the most widespread Sufi *tariqat* (brotherhood) in the republic, the Kunta Haji – the traditional focus of opposition to Russian imperial and Soviet rule. The centrality of Islam was so paramount that the opposition adopted Islamic slogans too and used language that related to Islamic issues in order to demonstrate that Dudayev was merely manipulating Islam for his own political ends.

After Dudayev was killed by a Russian rocket in April 1996, Chechnya continued to be the focus of radical Islamic activity. As acting president until Aslan Maskhadov's election in January 1997, Zelimkhan Yandarbiyev, the man who was thought to have introduced Dudayev to the possibilities of political Islam,[49] proclaimed the Chechen Republic of Ichkeria an independent Islamic state and took far-reaching steps to introduce *Shari'a* rule. The Chechen constitution was amended to read: 'Qur'an and *Shari'a* are the principal sources of legislation'. Yandarbiyev rescinded the Russian and Soviet legal system, and replaced it with the *Shari'a*-based criminal code enacted in Sudan. Secular courts were replaced by a supreme *Shari'a* court and by regional

---

[49] Anatol Lieven, *Chechnya: Tombstone of Russian Power* (New Haven and London: Yale University Press, 1998), pp. 363–4.

Shari'a courts. These measures were accompanied not only by the traditional punishments meted out by such courts but also by attempts to compel Chechen women to don the *paranja* and by a campaign against the sale and consumption of alcohol. Within weeks of being elected, Maskhadov followed in Yandarbiyev's footsteps and issued a decree declaring total *Shari'a* administration. Parliament ceased functioning and a commission was set up to elaborate a new constitution based on the *Shari'a*. But there was a major gap between the theory that lay behind these measures and Chechen reality, for the population proved to be unready for life as prescribed by the *Shari'a*, crime continued to prosper and the opposition to Maskhadov flourished.[50] The result was a total breakdown of law and order that led in summer 1999 to the outbreak of the second Russian–Chechen war, just two years after the agreements that ended the first one.

Political Islam as a threat to law and order

On the whole, the role of politicized Islam seems to have had only moderate significance for the development of Islam in the CIS. There have been a number of reasons for this, such as the lack of any charismatic leadership (with the exception perhaps of Tajikistan's Turajonzoda) and the reservations of the national intelligentsias. Another factor has been the divisions in the ranks of politicized Islamists.

The most notable exceptions – the two regions where political Islam has clearly wielded major influence in the first decade or so since December 1991 – have been Chechnya and Tajikistan. Yet even in these places it is self-evident that multifaceted internal conflicts and a long history of Soviet repression, including forced migration and resettlement of large populations, have provided sources of leverage for Islamist political movements.[51] In this way, paradoxically, Islam's politicization has emanated directly from the heritage of Soviet policy.

[50] Akaev, 'Religiozno-politicheskii konflikt v Chechenskoi Respublike Ichkeriia', pp. 101–8, and Bobrovnikov, 'Mythologizing Sharia Courts', p. 25. In Ingushetia too *Shari'a* courts were legalized. In December 1997, President Ruslan Aushev decreed that judges were to follow *adat* (customary law) and *Shari'a* norms in settling criminal and civil cases, and *Shari'a* norms relating to marriage and feuding were legalized.

[51] The entire Chechen population was, as noted above, deported in 1944 to Central Asia and returned only after the 1957 decree allowing most of the deported nationalities to return to their native parts. For the Islamic factor in the early stages of Chechnya's struggle for independence from Russia, see L.R. Polonskaia, 'Islamskaia legitimatsiia sovremennykh gosudarstvennykh struktur musul'manskogo mira (na primere SNG)', in *Sovremennyi islam: kul'tura i politika* (Moscow: Institut Vostokovedenie, RAN, Rossiskii Tsentr strategicheskikh i mezhdunarodnykh issledovanii, 1994), pp. 49–53. In Tajikistan the Garmis, who had been the victims of large-scale Soviet resettlement projects, were the main source of strength of the IRP. A Garm Islamic Republic was even proclaimed in Karategin in autumn 1992, and it existed until it was suppressed by government troops in February 1993.

Another exception may be the Fergana Valley, which has the densest population of all areas of Uzbekistan (some 550 people per square kilometre) and about one-half of the country's population. Living conditions have long been difficult, and there has been a high rate of unemployment.[52] It is extremely hard to gauge what in fact has been going on in the Fergana Valley since the crackdown by the authorities in spring 1992. Yet from such information as has circulated, it would appear that the towns of Andijan and Namangan and their environs have continued to be centres of Islamic activity with political connotations. President Karimov arrested alleged opponents there, on the grounds that they sought to undermine his regime by inciting Islamic fundamentalism. The persecutions began in autumn 1993, increased in momentum in summer 1994 and continued thereafter in fits and starts (see Chapters 6 and 8).

It seems evident that in endeavouring to assess the impact of political Islam and its potential as a threat to law and order, a distinction must be made between instances where it is to be found within government and those where it is in opposition. Its ability substantially to threaten the status quo must surely be much more considerable in the former cases, as Tajikistan and Chechnya have shown. Here Islamic players have had far greater leverage than they would have as pretenders to political power. At the same time, it must not be assumed *a priori* that the propaganda of Karimov, the Dagestani government and others who have used the danger of Islamic 'extremism' and fundamentalism to legitimize authoritarian regimes and destroy all opposition is necessarily totally unfounded. Just as it must not on any account be taken at face value, so it cannot be peremptorily dismissed. A contingent of the Islamic Movement of Uzbekistan did make incursions into Kyrgyzstan in summer 1999 and into Uzbekistan in summer 2000, and contingents of the Islamic Jamaat of Dagestan (see p. 45) made incursions from Chechnya into Dagestan in mid-1999 together with radical Chechen field commanders (see Chapter 8). These instances cannot be seen simply as attacks by military bands, for the two movements represent political forces whose goals are primarily political and are linked to both domestic Islam and the domestic political scene. In this way, by the end of the 1990s political Islam, whose radicalization had been precipitated by regime oppression, did seem to be threatening existing regimes both in Central Asia and in the North Caucasus. Whether or not one can legitimately talk of this phenomenon as a self-fulfilling prophecy, it gave rise to important political developments in both these regions and changed the balance of power within the CIS. It provided the backdrop against which Central Asia's new states were brought into a renewed dependence on Russia, and the second Chechen war was launched.

---

[52] Babadzhanov, 'The Fergana Valley: Source or Victim of Islamic Fundamentalism?', p. 127.

5 REGIONAL ATTRIBUTES AND DIFFERENCES

The CIS comprises a vast territory and the development of Islam has necessarily been very different in its various areas. Even under the Soviet regime, despite the homogeneity of the institutional apparatus which governed the country and the uniformity of the legal system, Islam took on fundamentally different forms among the motley of union and autonomous republics with Muslim populations. Indeed, major variations in Islamic practice pertained in many of these republics, most of which did not comprise historically distinct ethno-cultural entities.[1] These differences among and within the USSR's many Muslim regions derived from their dissimilar historical evolution and cultural and social heritage, and were exacerbated by the circumstances which accompanied the disintegration of the Soviet Union. Some territories became independent states; others remained subordinate to Moscow. None were monolithic in their attitude to Islam or to the phenomenon of an Islamic resurgence. For the purpose of this chapter, a few of the most crucial issues will be looked at, such as the status of the *Shari'a* and the use of violence.

Although a study of this nature cannot survey in depth all of the regions with major Muslim populations, it can take a cursory look at some of them in order to understand the wide range of possibilities for Islam's evolution in the CIS. The most important areas are the four which have been designated as the most intensely Islamic, namely the two independent states of Tajikistan and Uzbekistan, and the two republics of the Russian Federation, Dagestan and Chechnya, where the threat from Islam to the existing regime has been most conspicuous. By way of comparison, one or two less intensely Islamic states and republics will also be surveyed.

Tajikistan

Tajikistan had the distinction of being the only CIS state in the 1990s in which a Muslim political party seemed to constitute a genuine alternative to the dominant regime and actually participated for a while in government. The Islamic Revival Party

---

[1] For the diverse origins, history, culture and development of the USSR's Muslim peoples, see Shirin Akiner, *Islamic Peoples of the Soviet Union* (London: Kegan Paul International, 1983); and Alexandre Bennigsen and S. Enders Wimbush, *Muslims of the Soviet Empire: A Guide* (London/Bloomington, IN: Christopher Hurst and Indiana University Press, 1986).

of Tajikistan was a member of the coalition government in 1992 and, in its new guise as the Islamic Revival Movement, comprised the senior component of the United Tajik Opposition which was co-opted into government following the reconciliation agreement that ended the civil war in 1997. While its achievements served to raise a hue and cry in Uzbekistan, Russia and elsewhere concerning the danger of Tajikistan becoming an Islamic republic, this was not at any time a real component of the IRPT's programme, which assigned this ultimate goal to an indefinite future. Nor did the party at any stage pose a threat to the existing regime, except in the spring of 1992.

Insofar as Islam presented a danger to the regime in Tajikistan, it emanated from the strong Islamic character of Tajik society and everyday life. Thus, in regions where the mass of the population was hardest hit economically after independence, notably in Karategin, where, in addition, the local elite experienced frustration at being excluded from the national leadership, it was natural for dissatisfaction to take on an extreme religious form in the early and mid-1990s. Yet by the end of the decade radical Islamism no longer posed a serious threat; following the protracted civil war, the immediate need of the population was to return to normality and reasonable living conditions. Nonetheless, the proximity to Afghanistan, and the barely existent border with it,[2] made it impossible for any Tajik government to be totally sure of its immunity to Islamic radicalism, especially in the wake of the Taliban's successes. The constant contact between the two populations had become an especially acute issue in the context of the Tajik civil war and the influx of refugees from Tajikistan into Afghanistan. (There were thought to be between 100,000 and 120,000 refugees early in 1995, quite a few of whom mobilized in IRM fighting units; subsequently most seem to have returned to Tajikistan.[3]) Moreover, religion continued to play a role in regional rivalries within a country which was historically composed of disparate elements and seemed to many observers to be in constant danger of disintegrating.

Uzbekistan

The situation in neighbouring Uzbekistan was more complex. President Islam Karimov's regime was from the start obsessed about the potential threat from Islamic extremists. While able to suppress secular political parties and rivals, it found the Islamists far more difficult to manage. From time to time arrests were made of their leaders and activists, especially in various towns of the Fergana Valley (see Chapter 4), yet within a short period others took their place. It has not been objectively established that all subversive activity attributed to Islamic 'extremists' was in fact

[2] S. Olimova and M. Olimov, 'Tajikistan: Afghan Migration', *Russia and the Moslem World*, no. 5 (95), 2000, p. 27.
[3] Murat Laumulin, 'Tsentral'naia Aziia i situatsiia v Afganistane', *Tsentral'naia Aziia*, no. 1 (7), 1997, p. 47.

their doing, nor indeed that every alleged instance of such activity actually took place, yet Karimov has insisted that 'Wahhabis' and 'fundamentalists' stood behind virtually all violations of law and order (see Chapter 6). Certainly Islamists were the backbone of the events in Namangan in the winter of 1991–2 (see Chapter 4).

As in Tajikistan and the other Central Asian states, there have always been major differences in the nature and situation of Islam in Uzbekistan's various regions as a result of both ethnographic and historical conditions. In many ways the capital, Tashkent, and Bukhara are the most important Islamic centres, for they boast Islam's main administrative and academic institutions. But, whereas Islam in the country's main urban centres has had a relatively stable character, this has not been the case, as already noted, in the Fergana Valley, traditionally the most dynamic Islamic area of Uzbekistan. Even within the Fergana Valley there are major differences, with Namangan taking the lead in all that relates to Islamism. It has been suggested that the keenness of the Islamic opposition in the valley, and in Namangan particularly, has to be linked, as in Tajikistan, to the frustration of the regional elite at being passed over in the distribution of power at the national level.[4]

The Islamic radicalism that developed and surfaced in the region in the first years of the 1990s seems manifestly to have been a result of local conditions, attitudes and needs, for instance in its focus on the community and its structures. This was no longer the case towards the end of the decade when Islamic extremists from the Fergana Valley were again raising their heads. This time, however, the most militant activity came from outside Uzbekistan, where the leaders of the Islamic Movement of Uzbekistan had taken refuge. Moreover, the activity of Hizb al-Tahrir within the confines of the Fergana Valley (see Chapter 4) does not appear to be based on traditional social structures.

Dagestan

Unlike most Soviet republics, Dagestan had no titular nationality. It was comprised of a large number of indigenous ethnic groups, eleven of which were designated the country's major nationalities. Its ethnic heterogeneity, among other factors, was conducive to a variety of religious traditions, although the great majority of the peoples of Dagestan professed Islam. Most belonged to the Shafi'i *madhhab*, and Sufi brotherhoods were strong among them. Dagestan was generally considered the most Islamic of all the Russian Federation's republics and regions. Towards the end of the 1990s over 60 settlements in Dagestan were said to be living under *Shari'a* rule, although only the few villages dominated by the Wahhabis (see below) proclaimed

[4] Keith Martin, 'Kuda idut islamskie radikaly Tsentral'noi Azii?', *Tsentral'naia Aziia i Kavkaz*, no. 4 (5), 1999, p. 91.

this openly.[5] In the Avar region of northwest Dagestan, many of the large *kolkhozes* (collective farms) of the Soviet period broke up and reorganized along the lines of pre-revolutionary village communities or *jamaats*. By the mid-1990s the religious leadership in these communities was fulfilling the rights and functions of the *kolkhoz*, or local, administration. It saw to the rotation of crops, to the mending of roads and bridges and to canal irrigation and it collected fines and taxes. Every Friday it resolved local lawsuits in the mosque in accordance with the *Shari'a* and the *adat*, and passed judgment on villagers guilty of drunkenness, brawling and other minor offences. (In these parts major crimes requiring the intervention of the secular authority were rare.) The *Shari'a* courts settled 'small inheritance and criminal cases including divorce, theft, drinking alcoholic beverages, and the like', imposing fixed *Shari'a* and non-Islamic penalties. Their decisions were 'final and not subject to appeal', and there have been frequent instances of chairmen of village and district administrations calling upon local *qazis* (Islamic judges) to resolve a variety of disputes.[6]

Ahmad-qadi Akhtayev, a member of the largest Dagestani nationality, the Avars, was elected chairman of the All-Union IRP in 1990. That party had a disproportionately high percentage of Dagestani adherents and supporters, and its Dagestani affiliate called for the unity of Dagestan's peoples and that country's eventual transformation into an Islamic state (see Chapter 4). Dagestanis also made up the core of the Russian Union of Muslims (see Chapter 4), whose chairman was another Dagestani, Nadir Khachilayev. The party sought specifically to resolve all issues within the framework of the constitutions of the Russian Federation and Dagestan. As for Nur, the rival of the RUM, it set up an affiliated organization in Dagestan whose programme included preparing the groundwork for the introduction of *Shari'a* courts in Dagestan side by side with state courts, should defendants wish their cases to be reviewed in the former. Another organization which set up a branch in Dagestan was the All-Russian Islamic Congress, which came into being in early 1999. Its charter claimed it would represent 'in the political sphere the interests, views and desires of that sector of the population which shared the ideas and values of Islam' and take part in Dagestan's spiritual, cultural, economic and political revival.

The large number of Muslim organizations in Dagestan (for others besides those mentioned here, see Chapter 4), as on the all-Russian level, testified to their fundamental weakness, their inability to consolidate the ranks of their target audience. Another cause of inadequacy has been the gulf between them and the mass of the population. None of the Muslim movements were represented in the republic's state

---

[5] *Express Chronicle*, 13 September 1999, quoted in *Turkistan Newsletter*, 16 September 1999.
[6] Bobrovnikov, 'Islam i sovetskoe nasledie v kolkhozakh Severno-Zapadnogo Dagestana', p. 137, and Bobrovnikov, 'Mythologizing Sharia Courts', p. 25. The most comprehensive and up-to-date study of Islam in post-Soviet Dagestan is Makarov, *Ofitsial'nyi i neofitsial'nyi islam v Dagestane*.

organizations, although the deputy chairman of Dagestan's Muslim Spiritual Administration (DUMD) had a seat in parliament until the March 1999 elections. Certainly, Islam in Dagestan appeared as a divisive rather than a unifying force: there were major disagreements between clergy and believers and between clergy on the one hand, and the state and the secular political parties, on the other, with the clergy (and the Islamic parties) contemplating the establishment of an Islamic republic in Dagestan. There were also disagreements among the clergy: each of the major ethnic groups set up its own autonomous spiritual administration.

This divisiveness took on its most extreme form in connection with the growth of Wahhabism in Dagestan. By the mid-1990s, the disputes between the Wahhabis and the traditionalist Muslims extended well beyond issues of dogma. In the four districts where the former were concentrated, confrontations were so serious that in 1996–7 they sometimes deteriorated into armed clashes.[7] They almost certainly were responsible for the killing in 1998 of the mufti of Dagestan, Said Muhammad Abubakarov, who had both come out openly against Wahhabism, which he called 'pseudo-Islam', and criticized the republican leadership for not taking decisive measures against the Salafis, thus inciting 'interethnic and inter-confessional dissension'.[8] At the same time, the Wahhabis, or Salafis, were not a monolithic group, in Dagestan or anywhere else. The largest and most influential group were the adherents of radical Salafiyya headed by Bahauddin Muhammad, who called themselves the Islamic Jamaat of Dagestan. Even it, however, lacked any centralized organization, representing rather a conglomerate of separate *jamaats* that were united by certain common basic ideas, but not concurring on all issues.[9] According to one source, the tensions that were building up within the Muslim community between traditionalists and fundamentalists were exacerbated by Dagestan's economic decline and high rate of unemployment. As a result, many young men were attracted to military training camps in Chechnya run by Jadib Abd al-Rahman Khattab (known simply as Emir Khattab) and Shamil Basayev.[10] (Khattab, a Jordanian national of Chechen origin, had fought with the Afghan *mujahidin* against the Soviet invaders, and some time after the Soviet withdrawal in 1989 had moved to Chechnya.)

A majority of Dagestanis appear to have been disconcerted by the Wahhabi rejection of all political authority and by the support the Dagestani Wahhabis were

---

[7] For the evolution of antagonism between the Wahhabi 'reformers' and the traditionalists, see Bobrovnikov, 'Islam i sovetskoe nasledie v kolkhozakh Severno-Zapadnogo Dagestana', p. 138.

[8] Akaev, 'Religiozno-politicheskii konflikt v Chechensko Respublike Ichkeriia', p. 105; and Shikhsaidov, 'Islam v Dagestane', pp. 111–13.

[9] Makarov, *Ofitsial'nyi i neofitsial'nyi islam v Dagestane*, pp. 31–2.

[10] Enver Kisriev and Robert Bruce Ware, 'Conflict and Catharsis: A Report on Developments in Dagestan following the Incursions of August and September 1999', *Nationalities Papers*, vol. 28, no. 3, 2000, p. 479.

receiving from Chechnya. The latter factor brought to the surface a persistent undercurrent of anti-Chechen sentiment, the crux of which lay in deep-seated differences between the Dagestani social structure based on the *jamaat* and that of the Chechens based on an elaborate kinship system. The former is a well-knit community, 'organized politically and defined along territorial and historical lines', in which kinship concerns are subordinated to 'the political integrity of the community'. The announcement by the Chechnya-based Wahhabi insurgents that their incursions into Dagestan in August–September 1999 were part of a campaign to unite the highlanders of Dagestan with their Chechen allies against Russian imperialism rallied Dagestani public opinion behind the republican leadership.[11] The image of Wahhabis as traitors was reinforced by the international financial assistance they received, the international education of their youth, their operation of a satellite link in Kizilyurt and the foreign origin of some of their leaders and fighters.

Although it was supported by a mere 3 per cent of the population of Dagestan in spring 1999, Wahhabism's political significance was considerable, especially in rural areas, and it often divided families and villages into 'irreconcilable camps'. On the one hand, in the words of two scholars of the region, its 'rigid puritanism and fully veiled women were both alien and offensive to that free-wheeling, hard-drinking, roughshod egalitarianism with which Dagestan's traditional Islamic authorities had long since learned to compromise'.[12] On the other hand, it had a radicalizing effect on the Islamic establishment, which responded to Wahhabi criticism by becoming more puritanical and, to the deterioration of the political situation, by joining forces with the republic's secular leadership.

The Wahhabis recruited their adherents from diverse sources. Impoverished villages were attracted by Wahhabism's clarity and ideological simplicity as against North Caucasian Islam's 'cumbersome and often costly pseudo-traditions'. It 'lent dignity to the harsh austerity of their lives and provided spiritual sanction for their desperate hatred of Dagestan's wealthy new leaders'. A number of prosperous villages were drawn to Wahhabism's puritanism, which provided 'an organizational power for the preservation of their civic conventions and traditional morality against [the] degenerative influences of the media, mass culture, individualism and liberalism'. Both religious young people, who had lost respect for the elderly, semi-educated traditional clergy, and the intelligentsia, who sought an ideological footing, were attracted too. By mid-1999 Dagestan was increasingly dominated by events in a virtually independent Wahhabi territory in its centre.[13] Nothing short of a major Russian military action in the wake

[11] Ibid., pp. 482–7.
[12] Ibid., pp. 491–2.
[13] For the Salafi takeover of this territory, see Makarov, *Ofitsial'nyi i neofitsial'nyi islam v Dagestane*, p. 43.

46

of the incursions of August and September 1999 could even hope to defuse the major dilemma Wahhabism posed for both Makhachkala and Moscow.[14]

Chechnya

Under the Soviet regime Islam had seemed to be a unifying factor in Chechen society, consolidating the population in opposition to Moscow, or at least those among it who rejected the path of compromise with the authorities. But as in Dagestan, Islam became a divisive element in the 1990s. This was the result, above all, of the antagonism which developed between the country's traditional Sufi brotherhoods and the Salafis or Wahhabis. Even the far-reaching measures taken by Yandarbiyev and President Maskhadov to introduce *Shari'a* rule (see Chapter 4) did not end the confrontation between the two trends. (Maskhadov himself was no extremist but he yielded to pressures from the extremists.) The hostility between the two sides led in 1998 to bloodshed in Gudermes, where the estimated losses were between 50 and 100. Maskhadov accused the Salafis of establishing parallel military and political structures which rejected subordination to government agencies. Certainly, they had established their own *Shari'a* courts, which stood counterposed to those set up at the president's initiative.

Maskhadov's opponents included field commanders, such as Shamil Basayev and Salman Raduyev, both of whom identified with Islamic radicalism and stood at the head of autonomous armies, and also Yandarbiyev, whom he had defeated in the January 1997 presidential election. Yandarbiyev accused Maskhadov of being apprehensive about the growing role of religion in society and of not having a clear-cut programme for consolidating Chechnya as an independent Islamic state. However, Chechnya's mufti, Ahmad Qadyrov, insisted to the contrary that the division taking place among the Chechens was the result of Yandarbiyev's pro-Wahhabi activity and his invitation in August 1996 to Bahauddin Muhammad, the leader of the Islamic Jamaat of Dagestan, to establish *Shari'a* rule.[15] The persistent relations between 'Wahhabis' in the two neighbouring republics was a major bane to both their regimes. It played a focal role in the outbreak of the second Russo-Chechen war, which was triggered by the infiltration of areas of Dagestan by Basayev's troops (see Chapter 8).

Kazakhstan

Islam in Kazakhstan has traditionally been less devout than in Uzbekistan and Tajikistan. Nonetheless, a major trend within the national regeneration of the 1980s and 1990s insisted on the place of Islam and Islamic values and morals in the national culture. This led to the surfacing in Kazakhstan of most of the manifestations of the

[14] Kisriev and Ware, 'Conflict and Catharsis', pp. 491–9.
[15] Akaev, 'Religiozno-politicheskii konflikt v Chechenskoi respublike Ichkeriia', pp. 102–8.

religious revival in the CIS of these two decades (see Chapter 3). Special importance was placed on education, as general ignorance of Islam was considered the root of the population's alienation from it, and on charity. As early as 1990 the League of the Muslim Women of Kazakhstan was formed with the aims of resuscitating the traditions of Kazakh family and daily life, rendering help to the unfortunate and providing girls with a religious education.[16]

The religious renascence in Kazakhstan has exceeded the usual confines of a revival in Sunni Hanafi Islam. Sufism has remained strong in the south, which historically has been more pronouncedly Islamic than the rest of the country, because of both its sizeable sedentary Uzbek population and the influence of Ahmad Yasawi's shrine in the town of Turkestan. And, in 1994, an Ahmadiyya community was established, allegedly under the influence of Pakistani emissaries.[17] By the year 2000 the Kazakhstani authorities reportedly revealed a much higher level of underground Islamic activity than had been imagined and began taking measures to contain religious 'extremism'. A lengthy analysis of the situation in other Muslim regions where Islam had become radicalized, undertaken by, or under the auspices of, the director of the Kazakhstan Institute of Strategic Research, concluded that Kazakhstan was next in line, that there was a real danger of it 'becoming inveigled in the zone of deployment of religious extremism and terrorism'. This was the result both of developments in neighbouring Central Asian states and on the far littoral of the Caspian Sea, where the groundwork had been laid for the 'long-term destabilization' of these countries, and of trends within Kazakhstan's own Muslim community. The latter comprised the marginalization of the clergy of the non-Kazakh ethnic groups and the regional interests of Kazakh Muslims, and included major differences in religiosity between the population of the south and east, and that of the north and west. The evolution of Muslim communities that would be independent of the country's spiritual administration would make them fertile ground for radical Islam which would resort to 'the ideology of religious extremism'.[18] (This concern may well have been the source of the pressure apparently applied by the secular authority on the incumbent mufti to resign in June 2000 and on the Muslim clergy to replace him by a layman, who it evidently hoped would be both more effective and more pliant.[19])

---

[16] See Babak, Vaisman and Vasserman (eds), *Political Organization in Central Asia and Azerbaijan*.

[17] The Ahmadiyya is a school or movement active particularly in South Asia.

[18] Ashimbaev and Shomanov, 'Politizatsiia islama na postsovetskom prostranstve', pp. 11–14.

[19] On the new mufti, who had been serving as a counsellor in the Kazakhstan embassy in Saudi Arabia since 1997 and prior to that had been deputy rector of Kazakhstan State University, and the circumstances of his election, see *Delovaia nedelia* and *Novoe pokolenie*, 30 June 2000, and *Kontinent*, 29 November–12 December 2000. In an interview he gave to *Kazakhstanskaia pravda* (25 November 2000) he expressed his opposition to Islamic political parties and said that while the phenomena which led to Islamic extremism were absent in Kazakhstan, the government and the spiritual administration must not belittle the danger and must conduct a well-considered policy.

Tatarstan

In Tatarstan too Islam has been an integral component of the Tatar national revival. A Tatar national movement emerged under Gorbachev and grew in strength in the first years after the break-up of the USSR – when Tatarstan remained within the Russian Federation rather than becoming independent. Like Dagestan and Chechnya, it had been an autonomous, not a union, republic in the Soviet period. The movement's main goals were the strengthening of national consciousness, of which Islam was perceived to be an essential element, and the achievement of sovereignty. It was thus conducive to the formation of Islamic socio-political institutions and to the growth of a religious hierarchy (see Chapter 3), a significant minority of whom had obtained a religious education by the end of the 1990s, although the majority continued to follow popular Islam. Nonetheless, despite the consensus between the national, secular intelligentsia and the clergy about the need for a profound and multifaceted study of the Tatar heritage, the clergy have reached their own interpretation of socio-political concepts, phenomena and teachings. Whereas the intelligentsia have directed their attention to the 'Euro-Islam' of the Jadids (see Chapter 3), the clergy have tended to prefer traditionalist positions, which, they believe, are more likely to help consolidate traditional Tatar Muslim norms and institutions. This has been manifest in the debates concerning the adoption of the Latin alphabet, in which the clergy have suggested a return to the Arabic script.

The clergy themselves have not been united in their approach to a number of questions – despite agreeing on certain general objectives, such as the attainment of an improved social and juridical status for Islam and the *umma*. A principal issue on which there has been disagreement is the desirability of Islam's politicization. The Tatar mufti of the central All-Russia Muslim Spiritual Administration, Talgat Tajutdin, has persistently opposed all political activity by professional religious personnel, on the grounds that this divides the believer community. The new 'young imams', whose thinking developed under the influence of *glasnost*, have taken a contrary position, contending that in a heterogeneous multi-party society in which Muslims constitute a minority, they can defend their interests solely through political movements and parties. This has been one of the bones of contention between Tajutdin and the much younger mufti of Tatarstan, Gabdulla Galiullin.[20]

On the whole, the clergy in Tatarstan have opted for loyalty to both the central government in Moscow and the republican authorities in Kazan. They have preferred to seek to influence policy through cooperation rather than opposition and to strengthen their own position in society and the status of Islam through education rather than by resorting to violence. Unquestionably they have been aided in this by a moderate approach on the part of the authorities in both capitals.

[20] Mukhametshin, *Islam v obshchestvenno-politicheskoi zhizni Tatarstana*, pp. 95–125.

Another feature of Islamic life in contemporary Tatarstan has been a degree of tension between 'young imams' with positions in rural mosques and their parishioners. The latter have retained most of the customs and rituals of previous decades, which became over time increasingly divorced from orthodox Islam. They have been reluctant to give up their popular version of Islam for the more doctrinally correct positions their new pastors have imbibed in institutions of learning.

Summary

A brief survey of Islamic life and the situation of Islam in some of the regions of the CIS shows considerable differences but also evident similarities. Some of the latter result from the shared Soviet heritage, others from social, economic and political trends that tend to be similar in most areas of the CIS as its various regions seek to cope with their new political reality. The differences too have several sources: diverse traditions and customs, varying outside influences and also dissimilar political constellations resulting from a wide range of government constraints and legislation.

6 GOVERNMENTS AND ISLAM

One of the basic components of the evolution of Islam in the CIS, as in the Soviet Union before it, has been the policy of the governments concerned. It has been noted that most of the leaders and officials who filled central roles in government in the decade following the break-up of the USSR had previously been party apparatchiks, some of them of high rank, and that they had assimilated many of the assumptions and much of the basic outlook of the Soviet regime. And although they have in many instances shown themselves to be rather flexible in their attitude towards economic issues, for example market reforms and privatization, this has not been the case concerning Islam. The reason seems to be that, being themselves secular intelligentsia, they have a major commitment to the values of 'modernization', and are convinced that Islam is inherently at variance with them. They hold Gorbachev's view that the Islamic revival that accompanied *glasnost* was a threat to internal stability and even national security.

Thus, even those among the new leaders who have adopted some of the external trappings of Islam, seeing their people's faith as part of their national heritage, are not prepared to face the implications of an Islamic renascence. Above all, they are not ready to countenance Islamic activity over which they have no control. Like their Soviet predecessors, while preaching the separation of state and church, they have created administrative machinery to ensure that all religious activity will be subject to government supervision and surveillance. This was one reason why Karimov endorsed the establishment in Tashkent of an international centre for Islamic studies and an Islamic university and that his government sponsored an Islamic television station.[1]

The Soviet regime had created two institutions to implement its control of Islam. The first was the Council for Religious Affairs. This was in effect a government ministry, which served as an intermediary between the regime and the various faiths it recognized as existing legitimately. Most of the council's personnel, especially its key figures, came from the security apparatus, where some of them had held senior positions; they were also party members. The second institution consisted of the

---

[1] For the decree establishing the Islamic university, see *Pravda vostoka*, 8 May 1999; for the university's consultative council, see *Pravda vostoka*, 10 June 1999.

official religious establishment, whose existence was postulated on cooperation with the secular authority. The Muslim establishment was headed by spiritual administrations, of which there were four – each catering to a different geographical region (see Chapter 1, n. 1). These administrations consisted of religious figures, who for one reason or another consented to operate in accordance with the rules laid down by the regime.

A number of the post-Soviet regimes created analogous hierarchies. Councils for Religious Affairs came into being in the independent Muslim states; some of them were even called by the name of their Soviet prototype. No longer subject to party bosses, they were mostly subordinate directly to the head of state, and their respective chairmen manifestly enjoyed their president's confidence. In Russia itself the apparatus that served the executive was comprised of several elements: 'self-administration' organs at regional councils, a government Commission for Religious Organizations, which had its parallel at the State Duma, and a presidential Council for Cooperation with Religious Organizations, set up in 1995. Although the Russian Orthodox Church was the predominant influence in these organizations, some of the Muslim spiritual administrations were also represented. The central Muslim figure was Ravil Gainutdin, in his dual capacity as mufti of the Spiritual Administration of the Muslims of European Russia and chairman of the Council of Muftis of Russia.[2]

The situation was more complex when it came to the Muslim spiritual administrations. Already under Gorbachev two processes had begun which made state control of them significantly more difficult. The first was public protest against muftis (as the heads of the administrations were called), whose collaboration with the secular authority was accompanied by apparent disdain for traditional Islamic values. The first public demonstration to occur in Uzbekistan under Gorbachev, in February 1989, demanded the removal of Shamsutdin Babakhan from the chairmanship of SADUM (the Spiritual Administration of the Muslims of Central Asia and Kazakhstan). The authorities complied and a *qurultay* (convention) of Muslim religious figures replaced him with Muhammad Sodyk Mamayusupov (see Chapter 2). In the same year a similar demonstration in Buinaksk in Dagestan succeeded in having the mufti of the North Caucasian spiritual administration replaced. The new muftis were markedly less compliant – so much so that in 1993 Mamayusupov was compelled to go into exile.

The second process was the fragmentation of the spiritual administrations. As the union and the autonomous republics became increasingly independent and nationally oriented, they insisted on having their own spiritual administrations, each headed by a mufti. The first to do so in Central Asia was Kazakhstan in early 1990. Once this tendency took root, it proved to be a Pandora's box, and non-ethnic administrative

---

[2] Bobrovnikov, 'Islamophobia and Religious Legislation in Daghestan', p. 148.

units also began setting up autocephalous spiritual administrations, so that no fewer than 72 of them existed in the Russian Federation alone by the end of the 1990s. President Putin has tried to reinstate an all-Russia administration in order to recover state control of Islam, but as many of the administrations came into being precisely because they rejected domination by the central body, his efforts have so far (late 2000) been singularly unsuccessful.

In Dagestan the DUMD (the Spiritual Administration of the Muslims of Dagestan) was at one stage more effective in its struggle to recover the position it had lost upon the creation of other, ethnically based spiritual administrations (see Chapter 5). It managed in 1995 to subordinate all registered Muslim communities by erecting a hierarchy of mosque councils (*shuras*), whose supreme body was established at DUMD. It organized a strong lobby in the republican parliament through the Islamic Party of Dagestan (see Chapter 4), to which its leaders belonged, and was thus able to lobby for legislation relating to religion. It also participated in initiating the formation in 1998 of a Coordinating Centre of the Muslims of the Northern Caucasus, uniting the spiritual administrations of Dagestan, Ichkeria, Ingushetia, Kabardino-Balkaria, Karachaevo-Cherkessia, Stavropol, Adygei and Northern Ossetia-Alana to 'stand in the way of forces that want to detach the Northern Caucasus from Russia'. However, the March 1999 elections to the People's Assembly revealed that DUMD had lost its popularity, and neither its deputy chairman, who had hitherto been a member (see Chapter 5), nor other religious figures linked with it won seats.[3]

In the more compact independent Muslim states, most of which remained considerably more authoritarian than Russia from the very outset, the state has been able to retain its hold on the registered mosques and clergy through a single spiritual administration. In strict Soviet tradition it packed the muftiate with loyal clerics to whom it assigned considerable powers of jurisdiction. In Turkmenistan, President Niyazov preferred to establish a qaziate, headed by Nasrulla ibn Ibadulla, whom he also appointed as chairman of the Committee for Religious Affairs.[4] In Tajikistan the muftiate was abolished and replaced by a council of *ulamas* (clerics), which was headed by a former propagandist of atheism. And in Kazakhstan in the year 2000 a layman was actually appointed mufti (see Chapter 5). The state has also exerted direct control over registered mosques and the content of prayer meetings, issuing instructions via the local bureaucracy advising imams to criticize opposition figures and praise the regime. Imams have compared the new governments' methods with those of the old KGB and perceive the post-independence level of observation by security agents to be greater than in Soviet times. In Uzbekistan imams have been

[3] Ibid., pp.146–7, and Shikhsaidov, 'Islam v Dagestane', p. 112.
[4] Shahram Akbarzadeh, 'National Identity and Political Legitimacy in Turkmenistan', *Nationalities Papers*, vol. 27, no. 2, June 1999, pp. 283–5.

warned explicitly that disagreement with the government line could lead to arrest.[5] All the efforts of the secular authorities notwithstanding, a very considerable unofficial, popular Islam has persisted in all the Muslim states and has remained beyond the government's immediate control.[6] In Tajikistan the secular authority actually sanctioned certain forms of popular Islam, specifically Sufi activity in the Karategin area.

The governments' policy has been even more explicit in the legislation they have initiated than in the administrative machinery they have set up, ostensibly in order to ensure the implementation of the law. The major difference here, perhaps, between the Soviet era and the post-Soviet period has been that, on the whole, laws since 1992 have not been designed actually to curb religious worship and practice. Laws, as distinct from their implementation, have often been relatively lenient, indeed seemingly liberal and democratic. The prototype for this legislation was the RSFSR Supreme Soviet's 1990 law 'On Freedom of Conscience and Religious Organizations', which was incorporated into the Constitution of the Russian Federation of 1993. This law put an end to restrictions on the construction and opening of prayer houses and religious schools, the dissemination of religious literature and even foreign missionary activity. (As usual in the Soviet Union, the RSFSR's autonomous republics' Supreme Soviets followed suit with analogous legislation.)

The transformation of policy towards Islam has occurred because regimes are no longer committed to a materialist ideology which sees religion as a subversive element whose total elimination is an indication that the Marxist-Leninist prophecies are approaching fulfilment. On the contrary, at least in the states with Muslim titular nationalities, heads of state have associated themselves with some of Islam's precepts and customs. They have, for example, made the *hajj* or at least visited Mecca and taken their oath of office on the Qur'an, while Muslim festivals have become state holidays.[7] The major objective in law-making has become to restrict, if not actually prevent, political organization on the basis of Islam. Most states have prohibited the formation of religious political parties: in Uzbekistan there have been two laws to this effect, the first in 1992 (Article 57 of the Constitution), the second in 1997.

The more positive attitude of the post-Soviet governments towards Islam has been evident in their use of it to legitimize their policy, or certain aspects of it. When the

---

[5] *Central Asia: Islamist Mobilisation and Regional Security*, p. 14.

[6] The Kazakhstan Spiritual Administration, for instance, has not been able fully to control the situation even regarding the regular Hanafi mosques, many of which have developed independently from the centre. 'Sovremennaia religioznaia situatsiia v Respublike Kazakhstana', p. 63. In what are probably the two most intensely Muslim provinces – Jambyl and Southern Kazakhstan – at least half of the functioning mosques in the year 2000 were unregistered (129 of 258 in the former and 286 of 495 in the latter). *Novosti nedeli*, 7–13 November 2000.

[7] For instance in Uzbekistan. Abdullaev, 'Islam i "islamskii faktor" v sovremennom Uzbekistane', p. 87.

presidents of Uzbekistan, Turkmenistan and Kazakhstan undertook the *hajj* or took their oath of office on the Qur'an, they did so in order to indicate, even highlight, their association with the national faith. In this way they hoped to enhance their credentials and to gain support for what might otherwise seem to be an unalloyed anti-Islamic campaign. In the case of Turkmenistan, where Sapurmurad Niyazov has been making every effort to strengthen the Turkmens' national – as against traditional tribal – consciousness, the significance of Islam as a cornerstone of Turkmen identity has been stressed consistently. His senior Muslim factotum declared that 'mosques must become not only places of worship and *namaz*, but also centres for propagating the cultural legacies of our people'.[8] Also, prayers begin with praise to the Turkmenbashi.[9]

Yet even the government of Turkmenistan has not been able completely to dictate its terms to the Muslim clergy. It too was obliged to take administrative measures in order to reassert control. A re-registration of mosques in 1997 resulted in more than one-half of them not meeting requirements and not being able to re-register. In 1995–9 almost all the institutions of Islamic learning so recently opened were closed down, leaving only the *madrasa* of the qaziate, and restrictions were placed on religious tuition at the mosques. Islamic literature was no longer imported. In early 2000 Niyazov demanded that Turkmen Muslims refrain from resorting to the *Hadith* (traditions of the Prophet), on the grounds that its texts were 'uncanonical' and contained contradictions, and ordered the burning of 40,000 copies of the Qur'an translated into Turkmen.[10]

Even before it became clear that the regimes in the Muslim successor states were incapable of completely controlling the evolution of Islam, it was evident that their association with it must by definition be extremely limited. The governments' source of authority, in their opinion, could not and must not lie in religion and its precepts. Their fundamental approach to Islam has first and foremost been one of caution and uncertainty. They have convinced themselves that in the CIS it has a tendency to become radical and that their prime objective in regard to it must be to prevent that eventuality, for extremism not only is uncontrollable but also can actually threaten their regimes. Having taken this position in principle, they mostly have not ascertained how far danger really exists for each of them. The reasoning behind their cautious

[8] Quoted in Akbarzadeh, 'National Identity and Political Legitimacy in Turkmenistan', p. 284.
[9] Dzhumaev, 'Tsentral'naia Aziia', p. 14. According to this same source, new *suras* are reported to have actually been introduced into the Qur'an. (The *suras* are the 114 sections into which the Qur'an is divided.) The addition of new *suras*, or even the introduction of authentic *suras* into the prayer service, which is extremely concise, in this case apparently from political considerations (but for any other reason too), would be a very far-reaching measure. But offering prayers on behalf of the ruler at Friday and festival prayer services is not an innovation, having been the rule in the Middle East and Central Asia throughout the Islamic period.
[10] *Kontingent* (Almaty), no. 9 (22), 3–16 May 2000, pp. 35–7. The *Hadith* is second only to the Qur'an in sanctity.

55

approach – whether they simply followed in the footsteps of their communist predecessors or really believed in the presence of an immanent danger or, most likely, found it politically convenient to present such a picture to their public and the world outside – makes little difference to this analysis. But whatever their motivation has been, almost all the USSR's successor states have adopted this point of view, and it has necessarily coloured their policy towards Islam.

The most extreme case probably has been President Islam Karimov of Uzbekistan. In addition to the conditions and context of his access to power (see Chapter 2), Karimov has stood for over a decade at the head of the most populous Muslim state in the CIS and the one which includes a major traditional focus of radical, anti-establishment Islamic activity, the Fergana Valley. Concerns which he developed on the basis of his own domestic circumstances were, moreover, exacerbated by developments in neighbouring Tajikistan and Afghanistan. Since the outbreak of the civil war in Tajikistan in 1992, Karimov's domestic and foreign policy have both been predicated largely on the continuance of an Islamic danger which might jeopardize his country's stability and that of the region at large. Early in the conflict the Uzbek president was instrumental in persuading President Yeltsin to increase the Russian military presence in Tajikistan and to participate actively in consolidating the rule of the para-communist, hard-line Rahmonov regime. He also exercised pressure on the presidents of two other neighbours, Nursultan Nazarbayev of Kazakhstan and Askar Akayev of Kyrgyzstan, to join in quelling the attempt of the opposition in Tajikistan – of which the IRPT was the backbone – to take power. Uzbekistan itself sent consider-able troop reinforcements into Tajikistan to this end. The second chapter of Karimov's book, *Uzbekistan on the Threshold of the Twenty-First Century*, written in about 1995, is entitled 'Religious extremism and fundamentalism'. Here he talks of the threat these 'excessive manifestations' pose to 'stability and security' and he goes into considerable detail to describe how these trends seek to 'undermine the confidence of believing Muslims in the reforming state.... Islamists are aiming to discredit democracy, the secular state and a multinational and multiconfessional society.'[11]

Karimov has not confined himself to words. His active repression of sundry groups and large numbers of individuals on the grounds that they espoused radical Islamism has not been equalled by any other leader in the CIS. After suppressing Adolat (see Chapter 4), he initiated mass arrests of independent clergy in 1993–4. The charges usually were possession of narcotics or weapons or misappropriation of funds. The planting of narcotics and weapons on religious leaders and political dissidents – yet another Soviet legacy – continues to be practised as a pretext for their persecution. In subsequent years, according to one scholar, 'virtually all influential

---

[11] Islam Karimov, *Uzbekistan on the Threshold of the Twenty-First Century* (London: Curzon Press, 1997), pp. 25–6.

independent-minded religious leaders have been arrested or removed from their posts, and even rank-and-file believers have been subjected to harassment'.[12] In the wake of the killing of four policemen in Namangan in late 1997, which Tashkent blamed on Wahhabis, hundreds of arrests were made and random searches carried out, particularly of young bearded men. Indeed a law promulgated on 1 May 1998 prohibited Islamic dress (such as the *hijab* or *paranja*) and the sporting of beards. Many mosques have been declared illegal and pressured to close down, and the activity of many imams has been prohibited as a result of stringent registration criteria.[13]

Uzbekistan's foreign minister accused Islamic groups in Pakistan and Afghanistan of training young Uzbeks and other Central Asians to carry out terrorist acts with the intention of destabilizing Central Asia and ultimately setting up Islamic states in the region, a charge his Pakistani counterpart denied. In May 1998 Karimov told parliament that Islamic guerrillas 'must be shot in the head'; otherwise 'Tajikistan will come to Uzbekistan tomorrow.'[14]

After the bombings of February 1999 (see Chapter 8), the scale of arrests became even more massive, reaching into thousands, if not tens of thousands. Fieldwork in the affected areas has shown that in 'virtually every family' people knew someone who had been harassed or arrested for alleged association with non-sanctioned Islamic groups. It has been suggested that the law enforcement agencies have been issued quotas to fill and rewards for detaining more people.[15]

Another republic where the authorities have been extremely radical in their repression of 'Islamism' has been Dagestan, traditionally one of the CIS's more religious enclaves (see Chapter 5). Its believer population has sought to protest against the low moral and professional standards of the establishment clergy. The Dagestani leadership has taken the path of ruthless political and administrative oppression of this popular protest movement, which has taken the form of Wahhabism or Salafiyya. In late 1997 the People's Assembly issued a ban on Wahhabi activity, which was followed in January 1998 by a government decree 'On immediate measures against religious extremism'. In its wake, Wahhabi leaders were arrested, their offices demolished and their periodicals banned. Bombings were systematically blamed on the Wahhabis, providing the pretext for further repression. The Dagestani ruling elite has an immediate interest in taking this line, for it is constantly endeavouring to disguise its own corruption and to impress upon Moscow its political indispensability, and it is well aware of the latter's allergy to Islamic fundamentalism and North

[12] Bohr, *Uzbekistan: Politics and Foreign Policy*, p. 28.
[13] *Human Rights Watch Publication*, vol. 10, no. 4, May 1998. See also *Central Asia Monitor*, no. 3, 1998, p. 128.
[14] Bohr, *Uzbekistan: Politics and Foreign Policy*, p. 29.
[15] *Central Asia: Islamist Mobilisation and Regional Security*, pp. 7 and 13.

Caucasian 'banditry'.[16] Nor is it always clear how far Dagestani government measures are taken independently of Moscow; it is certainly possible that the Russian Federation's central government has an interest in Makhachkala adopting a more far-reaching policy of repressing Islamic militants than that with which it is prepared to associate itself formally. Unquestionably, the federal centre has been anxious regarding an extremist Islamic danger in Dagestan. This has been behind the major assistance voted to improving social conditions in that republic, as Moscow has tended to attribute the growth of Wahhabism to Dagestan's low standard of living (87th out of the 89 regions of the Russian Federation in terms of economic conditions).

The policy of the Russian Federation's central authorities towards Islam has been equivocal. According to one scholar, this is the outcome of a difference of opinion among policy-makers. On one side are those who proclaim the threat of Islamic fundamentalism in the North Caucasus, particularly in Dagestan. On the other side, several figures have been sympathetic to Islam. Led by the former Minister for Nationality Affairs, Ramazan Abdulatipov, and RUM Chairman Nadir Khachilayev, they include Ingushetia's President Ruslan Aushev and Chechnya's Aslan Maskhadov. These politicians have all sought to differentiate between various extremist groups and figures and the Russian Muslim community and Islam as a whole, emphasizing that the latter two are basically moderate forces that in fact promote stability. It was on their instigation that the government of the Russian Federation supported the celebration in 1997 of the 200th anniversary of Imam Shamil's birth.[17] In summer 1998 the new presidential commission for withstanding political extremism, together with the head of the Federal Security Service (FSB) and the ministers of justice, internal affairs and nationalities, resolved that Wahhabism was not an extremist trend.[18]

Whatever the reason for the equivocal character of Russia's policy towards Islam, there has indisputably been a transformation in Moscow's official line. The situation created by the RSFSR's 1990 law ending restrictions on various religious activities (see above) changed radically in September 1997. After a serious struggle, the Duma passed a new federal law on the Freedom of Conscience and Religious Organizations, which was eventually signed by Yeltsin, after an initial veto. This law limits considerably the rights of the so-called non-traditional religious communities. They had to register annually over a 15-year trial period, and they had no right to material or other

---

[16] Yemelianova, 'Islam and Nation Building in Tatarstan and Dagestan', pp. 612–13. In other North Caucasian republics too there has been friction between Islamists and the local authorities. Following a fracas in which young Muslims in Nalchik, the capital of Kabardino-Balkaria, beat up the sons of influential bureaucrats, whom they accused of 'getting fat on government funds', the authorities arrested young bearded men and seized worshippers in mosques under the age of 45. Institute for War and Peace Reporting, *Caucasus Reporting Service*, no. 63, 22 December 2000.

[17] Bobrovnikov, 'Islamophobia and Religious Legislation in Daghestan', pp. 140–1 and 144–6.

[18] *Izvestiia*, 22 July 1998.

support from either the federal or the republican powers. Nor might they open religious schools or educate children in the faith, publish or disseminate religious literature or maintain contact with foreign missionaries. Finally, religious associations might be liquidated or banned for committing offences, such as 'undermining social order' and 'igniting social, racial, national or religious dissension or hatred among people'.

Dagestan's version of this new law did not imitate the federal prototype. It accepted the need to tighten state control over religious communities but was specifically structured to suit local conditions. Its main aim was to prohibit Wahhabis from having their own mosques and religious schools, publishing and disseminating religious literature and maintaining links with the Arab organizations which funded them. In practical application, it denied registration to any organization if a religious organization with the identical name existed on the same territory. As both Wahhabis and communities registered with the official Spiritual Administration of Dagestan's Muslims designated themselves *jamaats*, the implication was unequivocal.[19]

The manifest interest of the governments concerned (both the Muslim states and Russia) in highlighting the threat to internal and regional stability allegedly emanating from Islamic extremism has not been confined to administrative measures and legislation. They have used it as an excuse for strengthening the executive power at the expense of the legislature and the centre at the expense of regional and local government; and all the governments, despite their pro forma commitment to democracy and democratic procedures, have demonstrated their authoritarian and centrist tendencies. Further, invocation of the threat has often enabled these governments to make common cause with some of the more progressive groups within their own societies, who were becoming estranged by their autocratic policy-making. The apparent need to quell Islamic terror appealed to the secularized intelligentsia as well as the business and entrepreneurial sector.

The Islamic threat has also become a key component of foreign policy within the CIS. For Russia in particular, it has proved to be a major boon, enabling it to aspire to recover its imperial, great-power status. Historically Russia had posed as the saviour of Christendom against the Turks and Mongols, and in the 1990s at least some elements of the Russian leadership perceived the struggle against Islamism as a continuation of their country's traditional role. Reformers at home, they were willing to join hands with hardline Islamophobes in the Muslim states of the CIS.[20] In this way they both strengthened their position *vis-à-vis* the leaders of these former Soviet

---

[19] Bobrovnikov, 'Islamophobia and Religious Legislation in Daghestan', pp. 143–4.
[20] This aspect of Russian foreign policy has been dealt with elsewhere and will therefore receive only brief treatment here. See, for example, Atkin, 'Islam as Faith, Politics and Bogeyman in Tajikistan', pp. 261–4, and Irina Zviagelskaia, *The Russian Policy Debate on Central Asia* (London: RIIA, 1995), pp. 10–12.

republics, demonstrating to them that only with Russian assistance could they hope to overcome the dangers of Islamism, and proved their value to Western governments, which were similarly anxious about the spread of Islamic terror.

An appreciation of the foreign policy value in Moscow and in the capitals of the new Muslim states, which were no less eager to point up their similarity of interests with the Western industrial and financial giants, has encouraged them to underscore – if not actually to exaggerate – the danger. This often seems to have reached the level of intentional disinformation in order to press the point with foreign leaders within the CIS and in the international arena. The Islamic factor has certainly been an important component in the alignment of forces within the CIS. In addition to the collusion of Russia, Uzbekistan, Kazakhstan and Kyrgyzstan over the Tajik civil war in 1992, the political and security establishments of these five states have convened on several occasions to discuss the threat posed by Islamic extremism in general and the Taliban in particular. President Karimov has also met with Ingushetia's President Aushev for the same purpose.[21]

Despite instances of cooperation between the Central Asian states against the background of the 'Islamic threat', this has also at times heightened mutual disgruntlement. Over the years, this was particularly true for Kyrgyzstan, whose sovereignty was violated on a number of occasions as Uzbek security forces and intelligence pursued Uzbek Islamists on Kyrgyz territory. Mutual suspicion and differences of approach continued to undermine chances for effective cooperation even when the threat began to appear more real in 1999 and 2000.[22]

The incursion of radical Islamic Movement of Uzbekistan forces into Kyrgyzstan in 1999 (see Chapter 8) brought Uzbekistan back into line from Moscow's point of view after its defection from the CIS security pact and association with GUAM, the grouping of Georgia, Ukraine, Azerbaijan and Moldova designed to counter Russian hegemony.[23] (Uzbekistan has not, however, formally re-entered the CIS security pact and it has continued to reject the stationing of Russian troops or the establishment of Russian bases on Uzbek territory, although President Karimov concedes that Uzbekistan, while 'able to defend itself', needs to re-equip and modernize its armed forces.[24]) The cooperation between Russia and the four Central Asian states of Uzbekistan, Kazakhstan, Kyrgyzstan and Tajikistan has increased since the advent to power of Vladimir Putin, who used the 'Islamic threat' as a main slogan in his campaign for the

---

[21] Herzig, 'Islam, Transnationalism, and Subregionalism in the CIS', p. 245.

[22] *Central Asia: Islamist Mobilisation and Regional Security*, pp. 14, 15 and 21.

[23] For GUAM, see Boris Parahonskiy, 'The Formation of Regional Cooperation Models in GUUAM', *Central Asia and the Caucasus*, no. 2, 2000, pp. 73–9. The GUAM political and advisory forum was formed in October 1997 within the framework of a European Council summit. In April 1999 Uzbekistan joined the group, which was renamed GUUAM.

[24] *Vremia novostei*, 25 September 2000.

presidency and who has taken advantage of the panic among his Central Asian colleagues to reassert their dependence on Russia.

In Kyrgyzstan President Akayev stated in May 1998 that his country would cooperate with Russia, Uzbekistan and Tajikistan in the struggle against 'fundamentalism'. His spokesman said he was personally concerned about the 'appearance of Wahhabi missionaries' and the government ordered all mosques to register, thereby committing itself to 'keep track of who preaches and where they are from'.[25] Both Kyrgyzstan and Kazakhstan took measures in the wake of the events in the region in the subsequent two years to curb Islamic radicalism and 'extremism'. These steps included more restrictive legislation, administrative repression and military measures (see also Chapter 8).[26]

After a fairly promising start – except in Uzbekistan and Turkmenistan – both Russia and the states with Muslim titular nationalities have reverted to a more hardline policy towards Islam. In part, this has been the consequence of the traditional need of authoritarian regimes for internal and external enemies against whose threat they could try to legitimize extra-legal administrative actions and even repression, as well as to mobilize the bulk of the population. The more hardline policy makes a distinction between a legitimate national and cultural revival, with its inevitable use of Islamic symbols, customs and rituals, and an Islamism that seeks to make religion the focus and backbone of society in the new national state. All religious manifestations and associations that are not subordinate to the official Muslim establishment are by definition hostile to the state and its goals. Thus they have to be restricted and, where possible, eliminated.

[25] *Central Asia Monitor*, no. 3, 1998, p. 227.
[26] Kazakhstan, for example, has recalled all nationals studying at foreign institutes of Islamic learning except those sent by the country's official Muslim establishment. *Kazakhstanskaia pravda*, 25 November 2000.

7 ISLAMIC SOLIDARITY

One of the criteria for gauging the political implications of Islam for the CIS must be its capability for organizing and consolidating its ranks. Under the tsars and the communists, when the state voiced its worry about a Muslim threat, it spoke of pan-Islam, a movement or tendency for Muslims everywhere to unite under Islamic slogans. But this was never a real danger; indeed, it often seemed a parody, given the inexorable divisiveness of Islam and Muslim society in the late nineteenth and throughout the twentieth century. (Right up to the present day the only ranks Islam has served to consolidate have been those of its detractors, who have come together to fight it.) The trend towards fragmentation was hardly arrested by the appearance in the last third of the twentieth century of a number of international Muslim organizations which also have been frequently rent by internal divisions and conflicting interests.

Within the CIS

Within the CIS there has been very little in the way of pan-Muslim organization. The first exception was the All-Union Islamic Revival Party, which seemed for a very short while to promise a common platform for, and joint activity by, representatives of a number of the Soviet Union's Muslim ethnic groups – though not all of them sent delegates to the party's founding conference in 1990 (see Chapter 4). This effort at transnational mobilization was unable to sustain itself due to ideological and personal differences within its leadership and to the diverse circumstances of the several republics. These factors caused the IRP's republican branches to adopt varying strategies and tactics, and by 1994 the party had ceased to function as a single entity, although some of its splinter parties continued to exist.[1]

As of 1995 there were also Muslim political organizations in the Russian Federation (see Chapter 4). And these too were unsuccessful in combining Muslims: the very fact that almost from the start there were two parties was an indication of the improbability of Muslim solidarity or a single political organization representing Russia's Muslim peoples. Moreover, the majority of Muslims apparently do not

---

[1] Herzig, 'Islam, Transnationalism and Regionalism in the CIS', p. 241.

identify themselves paramountly as Muslim. They seem actually to prefer non-Muslim parties, which reflect their political, economic and social interests.

True, there have been ad hoc attempts to establish transnational Islamic movements for specific ends. One of these has been the Coordinating Centre of the Muslims of the Northern Caucasus (see Chapter 6). However, the purpose of this group of traditionalist clerics – to repress Wahhabism – highlights the fact that it cannot be taken as a focus of Islamic solidarity.

A further indication of the lack of solidarity among CIS Muslims is provided by some of the region's more traumatic experiences in the last dozen years of the twentieth century. With the advent of *glasnost* and the surfacing of national movements among the Soviet Union's Muslim nationalities, long-hidden grievances of one Muslim ethnic group *vis-à-vis* another became public. One of these was the bitterness Tajiks felt towards Uzbeks, resulting from the forcible registration of Tajiks in the Uzbek SSR, particularly in the Bukhara and Samarkand regions, as Uzbek nationals, which denied them access to their ethnic culture. There were even cases of violence among Muslims in the Gorbachev era. In 1989 Uzbeks massacred Meskhetian Turks in the Fergana Valley, and in Novyi Uzen in western Kazakhstan, Kazakhs committed a pogrom against Muslim Caucasian oil workers. In 1990 Kyrgyz and Uzbeks fought each other in Osh province in southern Kyrgyzstan. The violence was not only the result of ethnic rivalry or of grievances that took on an ethnic aspect. The civil war in Tajikistan was fought basically between Tajiks of different regions.[2] More recently, in Dagestan the republican establishment, representing the country's nationalities, all of whom are Muslim, has declared an open, all-out struggle against Islamic 'extremists' or 'Wahhabis'.

In the light of these conflicts within the Muslim community, efforts to create all-Muslim organizations and forums indicate the desire of certain elements to transform Islam into a unified social, economic and even political force; they do not actually reflect such a reality. The question that must be posed is whether a reinforcement of the Islamic identity of the Muslim ethnic groups may alter the picture radically. While greater unity is hardly on the cards for the very large Tatar population in Russia's cities, for example, or for Kazakhs in northern Kazakhstan, it may happen in regions where the titular nationality is Muslim and comprises a clear majority of the population. The former groups are not necessarily less inclined to identify themselves individually as Muslims, but they lack the official frameworks for expressing that identity collectively which exist in some Muslim regions. Moreover, as has been mentioned, most members of the CIS Muslim nationalities apparently identify themselves as Muslims but do not see the Muslim aspect of their identity as paramount. They do not perceive it as obliging them to take specific public action or as making

[2] See Shirin Akiner, *Tajikistan: Disintegration or Reconciliation?* (London: RIIA, 2001).

such action desirable. The secular intelligentsia's main ambition probably remains, as under Soviet rule, to become part of the mainstream of a modern, technological and pluralistic urban society. But the rural population and most of the urban lower classes have retained clan, tribal, regional and ethnic loyalties that seem to them more demanding and immediate. Islam to them is part of their more particularistic affiliations.

The first Chechen war was an issue which enhanced the Muslim consciousness of many Muslims of different ethnic groups within the Russian Federation and strengthened their sense of being different from their Christian neighbours. True, only a few of these Muslims volunteered to fight alongside the Chechens, and many seem to have been alienated by the image of Chechen extremism propagated by the Russian media, but the actions of the Russian army in Chechnya were a thorn in the side of any Russian–Muslim 'normalization' (cf. Chapters 4 and 6).[3] There have also been other instances of Muslims of one ethnic group fighting along with co-religionists from another group. One case was that of the Islamic Movement of Uzbekistan contingent which fled to Tajikistan, where it joined forces with the United Tajik Opposition. Moreover, on the occasion of the IMU incursion into Uzbekistan and Kyrgyzstan in August 2000 (see Chapter 8) the Kyrgyz defence minister said that among its fighters were not only Uzbeks but also Tajiks, Tatars and Bashkirs and that its field commanders included Chechens, Indians, Pakistanis, Afghans and Arabs.[4]

The Muslim world outside

Against the backdrop of the divisiveness of the Muslim nationalities and Islamic community within the CIS, the likelihood that CIS Muslims perceive their membership in the worldwide Muslim *umma* as a meaningful social or political factor in their collective existence must be slight. While they accept the belief in Islam's universality and re-affirm a variety of general Muslim issues, they view unity and universality primarily as part of culture and spirituality rather than actual politics.[5] The governments of the Muslim successor states, and a variety of organizations within them, have called specifically for links with the Muslim world outside, but they have done so primarily because they have felt that they might find a common language with some of its leaders who were experiencing similar problems and attitudes, or that they might obtain much-needed support. They have not been motivated by strictly Islamic considerations. Yet there has been some identification with 'Muslim causes'. For example, an official of the All-Tatar Public Centre remarked in 1999 that over 100

---

[3] For the participation in the second Chechen war of several hundred North Caucasians from different nationalities, see Chapter 8.

[4] APR (Agency of Political Research), 3 September 2000; *www.caapr.kz*

[5] Herzig, 'Islam, Transnationalism and Regionalism', p. 235.

Tatar nationals had visited his organization's offices and offered their services for Kosovo after NATO opened its Balkan campaign.[6]

At the same time, actual contacts with the Muslim world outside the borders of the CIS, which have increased markedly since *glasnost* and the USSR's disintegration, have in part had a specifically Islamic content. In the first place, there has been the *hajj* (see Chapter 3), which has brought tens of thousands of CIS Muslims into direct contact with Muslims from many countries and which, perhaps more than any other single circumstance, brings home to the pilgrim his participation in a universal Muslim occasion. Secondly, the number of CIS Muslims studying in Muslim countries, both in Islamic institutes and universities and in secular ones, has grown enormously (see Chapter 3), inevitably exposing them to Middle Eastern and South Asian Muslim thinkers and ideas. This has been reflected in calls for the establishment of a worldwide Islamic caliphate or for more limited manifestations of Islamic solidarity, such as a renewed Federation of the Caucasian Peoples, or at least a union of Chechnya and Dagestan in a restored Imamate of Shamil, and in Central Asia a restored Kokand Khanate or Musulmanabad. Thirdly, direct contacts and the transmission to and from the CIS of ideas, literature and even organizational frameworks, including those linked to Islam, have been further facilitated by transborder and émigré ethnic groups. There are large communities of Tajiks, Uzbeks and Turkmen in Afghanistan and of Uyghurs in Kyrgyzstan, Kazakhstan and Xinjiang, this Chinese province also being the home of a large Kazakh diaspora. Descendants of Chechens who left the Caucasus in the nineteenth century for various countries of the Middle East have returned to Chechnya, where one of them, Emir Khattab, has played a leading role in disseminating radical Islamism.[7] And fourthly, foreign Muslim governments and charitable organizations have contributed significantly to the Islamic revival throughout the CIS. They have introduced Qur'ans in Arabic and in the languages of some of the major CIS nationalities, and also other Islamic literature, particularly textbooks for the study of Islamic subjects. They have financed the construction of mosques and educational institutions, whose teaching personnel in many instances have come from abroad (see Chapter 3).

The Muslim countries with which there seems to have been most contact have been Iran, Turkey, Saudi Arabia and Afghanistan, but also Pakistan, Kuwait and the United Arab Emirates (UAE). This holds for both intergovernmental and other, less formal, ties. It is important to emphasize, as has already been noted, that 'the declared policies of all state actors prioritize respect for sovereignty, non-interference in

---

[6] *Christian Science Monitor*, 20 May 1999. It appears, however, that none actually went. Certainly, neither the Russian Federation nor the Tatarstan authorities were in favour of such a step, although the deputy head of Tatarstan's Muslim Spiritual Administration said he understood the link with a fellow Muslim minority dominated by Slavs.

[7] Herzig, 'Islam, Transnationalism and Regionalism', pp. 238–9.

domestic affairs and the development of state-to-state relations'. Insofar as there has been external support for radical Islamists within the CIS, it has been 'carried out by covert state or quasi-state actors',[8] or, according to Russian officialdom, by organizations, including extremist ones, which governments have difficulty in controlling. While 'representatives of Russian religious organizations' have reported the arrival of preachers, missionaries and tourists who were remote from politics, the Russian Federal Security Service (FSB) has contended the opposite. It has said that citizens of foreign Muslim countries have come as tourists, then have changed their status, stayed on as preachers, for example, and in this capacity have travelled around Russia creating terrorist organizations and enlisting people for a variety of tasks and training abroad.[9]

The West has been most concerned about the CIS Muslim states' links with Iran, although over the years these have, at least on the surface, taken on a relatively moderate character. The reasons for this are apparently twofold. On the one hand, radical Islam in the CIS has been Sunni rather than Shiite and has therefore not gravitated towards Iran; on the other hand, Iran's own policy towards the successor states has been mitigated by a host of considerations. The Islamic factor is but one of these, and hardly the most important one – it is probably relations with Russia.

In its ties with the Muslim states, Iran has acted on three levels – promoting regional alliances (see below), enhancing bilateral relations and encouraging and supporting radical Islamic movements. Both the government and the quasi-state Islamic foundations have sought, especially immediately after the Muslim successor states came into being, to 'lead, encourage and shape' their Islamic revival. This has involved constructing mosques, opening religious schools, distributing Qur'ans and textbooks, broadcasting Iranian radio and television, initiating the teaching of Farsi and training young clerics. Iran has also striven to increase its influence with radical movements. Although commentators do not totally agree about how much has been going on beneath the surface, it seems that even Iran's main effort has been directed towards enhancing intergovernmental relations and economic interests rather than promoting Islamic revolution.[10]

The one country that does have a Shiite majority, Azerbaijan, has had very little in the way of Islamic radicalism. However, Iranian preachers were active in the Gorbachev

[8] Ibid., p. 236.
[9] NTV in Russian, 25 November 1995; SWB (BBC Summary of World Broadcasts), 28 November 1995.
[10] David Menashri, 'Iran and Central Asia: Radical Regime, Pragmatic Politics', in David Menashri (ed.), *Central Asia Meets the Middle East* (London: Frank Cass, 1998), pp. 83–4, 89 and 93; Herzig, 'Islam, Transnationalism and Regionalism', p. 236; and also Edmund Herzig, 'Iran and Central Asia', Chapter 8 in Roy Allison and Lena Jonson (eds), *Central Asian Security* (Washington, DC/London: Brookings/RIIA, 2001), pp. 171–98.

period in some parts (notably in the countryside around Baku and in Lenkoran and Nakhichevan). Although Iranian influence receded after independence, it appeared to have made something of a comeback by the middle of the 1990s, and the leaders of the Islamic Party of Azerbaijan (IPA) were charged with spying on its behalf (see Chapter 4). President Aliyev's foreign policy adviser accused Iran in 1995 of expending large sums to 'propagate its fundamentalist variant of Islam' in Azerbaijan.[11] Following the trial of the IPA leadership, Iranian influence was again reduced to minimal proportions – the broadcasting of Iranian television was forbidden and Iranian missionaries were deprived of the right to operate in Azerbaijan.[12]

The other Muslim state where Iran was manifestly present in the immediate post-independence period was Tajikistan, because of the two countries' cultural and ethnic affinity. The Islamic opposition there, however, was oriented towards Afghanistan. Nonetheless, political émigrés from Tajikistan and Uzbekistan were reported to have taken refuge in Tehran over the years. One Uzbek scholar, who accepts that Iran's foreign policy became less ideologically oriented over the course of the 1990s, still contended at the end of the decade that Iran exercised considerable influence over the Tajik opposition and that in the event of its victory Tehran would obtain 'additional leverage' over the religious situation in Uzbekistan. In his view Iran continued to support Islamic political movements which operated illegally in Uzbekistan and to establish ties with Sufi orders.[13]

The Muslim successor states' strongest ties with any foreign country after independence were with Turkey. They perceived it as a model of a modernized Muslim state, which, moreover, maintained close relations with the West.[14] Turkey, for its part, emphasized its ethnic, cultural and linguistic affinity with these countries, especially Azerbaijan. Secularism being one of the manifest advantages of Turkey's modernism in the eyes of the Muslim states, neither side was interested in basing the relationship on Islam or Islam-linked themes.[15] Yet in the course of the 1990s, as the initial enthusiasm surrounding intergovernmental ties with Ankara cooled, the Turks too became more involved in Islamic affairs. Turkey was instrumental in mosque-building in a number of the Muslim regions of the CIS, notably Tatarstan and Azerbaijan. In winter 1996–7 Turkish builders completed a large mosque in Makhachkala and in spring 1997 Dagestanis could watch Turkish television programmes in which Islamic

---

[11] *Moskovskaia pravda*, 9 August 1995.

[12] Rotar, 'Islamic Fundamentalism in Azerbaijan: Myth or Reality?'.

[13] Abdullaev, 'Islam i "islamskii faktor" v sovremennom Uzbekistane', p. 96.

[14] See, for example, Reef Altoma, 'The Influence of Islam in Post-Soviet Kazakhstan', in Beatrice F. Manz (ed.), *Central Asia in Historical Perspective* (Boulder, CO: Westview, 1994), p. 170.

[15] For Turkey's relations with the Muslim successor states, see both Philip Robins, 'Turkey's Ostpolitik: Relations with the Central Asian States', and William Hale, 'Turkey and Transcaucasia', in Menashri (ed.), *Central Asia Meets the Middle East*, pp. 129–49 and 150–67. Neither article mentions any Turkish activity at all connected with Islam.

themes predominated.[16] Turkey also set up *madrasas*. It has been asserted that both the Foundation of Turkish Religious Affairs and, until the February 1997 coup in Turkey, the Directorate of Religious Affairs of Turkey were both extremely energetic in supporting Islamic institutions and activities in Central Asia.[17] The Spiritual Administration of the Muslims in Dagestan also sought ties with Turkey, in the international arena and in its educational programme, seeing in Turkish Islam with its traditional ties with Naqshbandi Sufism a potential counterweight to the spread of Wahhabism.[18]

As the guardian of Islam's holy places and a country with relatively few budgetary restraints, Saudia Arabia has been both keen and able to pose as the major external Islamic influence on the Muslim CIS states. It sponsored pilgrims, and in addition to providing Qur'ans and building mosques and schools, it has supported major relief programmes. As early as 1990, before the break-up of the Soviet Union, Saudi Arabia committed $1.5 billion to that country, most of it earmarked for religious and cultural ends. Saudi financial assistance to the Islamic revival has been channelled through governments and the official religious establishment.[19] Its rivalry with Iran over 'a global primacy of Islam' brought Saudi Arabia to Central Asia to thwart Iranian Islamic radicalism, but over time it has become no less, and perhaps even more, concerned about Turkish Islamic reformism.[20]

In addition to providing official assistance to Islamic activity, Saudi Arabia has been suspected, by the Russian government among others, of funnelling large sums to Wahhabis in the Northern Caucasus, particularly Dagestan, and conducting large-scale missionary activity there.[21] It was presumably in this context that when fighting broke out in Dagestan in August 1999 (see Chapter 8), the Saudi government reportedly approached Moscow with an official request not to call those seeking Islamic reform in Dagestan Wahhabis.[22] At the same time, some Saudis have unquestionably fought in Chechnya, although there is no way of estimating their numbers, and we must presume that they did not go there as official representatives of their government. Saudi Arabia has also been thought to support unorthodox Islam in Uzbekistan,

[16] Bobrovnikov, 'Islamophobia and Religious Legislation in Daghestan', p. 150.
[17] M. Hakan Yavuz, 'Turkish Identity Politics and Central Asia', in Sagdeev and Eisenhower (eds.), *Islam and Central Asia*, p. 208. For Turkey's initiative in establishing *madrasas* in Kyrgyzstan, see Chapter 3.
[18] Makarov, *Ofitsial'nyi i neofitsial'nyi islam v Dagestane*, p. 17.
[19] Herzig, 'Islam, Transnationalism and Regionalism,' p. 236; see also Chapter 3.
[20] David Menashri, 'Introduction: Is There a "New Middle East"?', in Menashri (ed.), *Central Asia Meets the Middle East*, pp. 14–15.
[21] Bobrovnikov, 'Islamophobia and Religious Legislation in Daghestan', p. 142. Bobrovnikov is convinced that the Russian government has seriously overestimated both the amounts of money and the scale of this missionary activity.
[22] Zagir Arukhov, *Ekstremizm v sovremennom islame* (Makhachkala: Agentsvo "Kavkaz," Redaktsiia analaticheskoi informatsii), p. 106.

notably in the Fergana Valley, devising special programmes for training religious personnel, providing literature and money and constructing mosques and *madrasas*.[23]

Other countries too have financed Islamic institutions and activity, if less intensely than the Saudis, notably Pakistan, the UAE and Kuwait.[24] Pakistan – thought, like Saudi Arabia, to want to counter Iran's activities in Central Asia – has joined it in financing the construction and repair of mosques in Uzbekistan.[25] Pakistan's support for the Taliban, which was said to be seeking the Islamization of Central Asia, has not been forgotten or ignored by the Muslim successor states of the region.[26] Members of the exiled opposition Islamic Movement of Uzbekistan (IMU) have actually been claimed by the Uzbek government to be receiving military training in Pakistan and Afghanistan (see Chapters 6 and 8). Indeed, the IMU does seem to have had to rely on external sources for its finances, equipment, training centres and bases and head-quarters (see below). In the course of the second Chechen war the Chechens found financial aid and fighting personnel both in Pakistan and in the Persian Gulf, notably from private institutions and individuals aiming to promote radical forms of Islam worldwide (see Chapter 8). On the whole, however, the response to appeals by Chechen leaders for help in their 'holy war' against 'infidel Russia' was meagre. The Pakistani government was the only Muslim government actually to intervene in Moscow, where it urged a peaceful solution in keeping with the fundamental rights of the Chechen people, although the Grand Mufti of Egypt had called upon all Muslim countries to cut political and economic ties with Russia and requested the inter-national community to intervene and stop 'collective massacres' committed by the Russian military.[27]

Certainly, the most complex and controversial external influence has been that of Afghanistan, whose impact has been both active and passive. It borders three Central Asian states and has a rather large co-ethnic population with all three; events there must necessarily reverberate in Central Asia, especially in Uzbekistan and Tajikistan. The civil war in Afghanistan, specifically the uprising of the *mujahidin* against the Marxist regime which took over the country in 1978, had a deep effect on the peoples of Soviet Central Asia. This effect was all the more profound because of the involvement of a considerable Central Asian, particularly Tajik, contingent in the

[23] Abdullaev, 'Islam i "islamskii faktor" v sovremennom Uzbekistane', p. 97.

[24] In 1998 the head of the Caucasian Islamic Centre in Makhachkala was arrested on charges of illegal possession of arms and maintaining contacts with a Kuwaiti citizen who headed the Wahhabi 'centre' in Baku. *Izvestiia*, 14 August 1999. For Kuwait and Saudi financing of Islamic universities in Moscow and Baku respectively, see Chapter 3.

[25] Abdullaev, 'Islam i "islamskii faktor" v sovremennom Uzbekistane', p. 96.

[26] Ibid., pp. 96–7.

[27] Eugene Rumer and Brenda Shaffer, 'An Islamist Challenge in Russia?', *Policy Watch*, no. 418, 25 October 1999; AFP, 15 November 1999, *www.iviews.com*; and *Al-Ra'y al-Amm*, 12 December 1999. I am grateful for these sources to Esther Webman of the Moshe Dayan Center at Tel Aviv University.

Soviet intervention in the war. And in the Tajik civil war, the very notion of an Islamic opposition taking up arms against a para-communist regime was imported directly from Afghanistan, along with much of the opposition's weapons. The open border between the two countries – neither the Soviets nor the Russian border troops in the 1990s were able to close it (see Chapter 5) – enabled a continuous flow of arms into Tajikistan. Fighters also crossed back and forth, and tens of thousands of Tajik refugees fled into Afghanistan as civil war racked their country in the 1990s. The bugbear that haunted the Central Asian governments was an 'Afghanization' or 'Talibanization' of Central Asia north of the Pyanj River (see Chapters 6 and 8). The Afghan leaders Burhanuddin Rabbani and Abdurashid Dustum, as well as the Taliban, were perceived as desiring some form of Islamization of Central Asia.[28] The Islamic Movement of Uzbekistan had an office in Kabul by the end of the 1990s, and some 2,000 IMU fighters were reported by Afghan sources to have received sanctuary just over the Uzbek border in the northern Afghanistan town Mazar-i Sharif.[29] The common interest of Russia and the Central Asian governments in fighting Islamic terrorists provided the backdrop for President Putin's threats to make a pre-emptive strike against training camps in Afghanistan.[30] The Central Asians rejected these threats, and by the year 2000, as Taliban forces won further victories and the Northern Alliance of the remaining opposition which Tashkent had supported lost ever more ground, Turkmenistan and Uzbekistan were negotiating with the Taliban, although refraining from granting their government formal recognition. (It has even been maintained that the other Central Asian governments have followed suit.[31])

Links of a very different nature have existed between Uyghurs in Kazakhstan and their compatriots over the border in the Chinese Uyghur Xinjiang Autonomous Region, whom they are thought to be supplying with arms and literature. Since the disintegration of the Soviet Union and the independence of the Central Asian states, three of which border on Xinjiang, Beijing has been concerned about separatist tendencies among the Uyghurs. It has taken severe repressive measures against Uyghur nationalists, and as a result large numbers of Uyghurs are said to have crossed into Kazakhstan. Like Russia and the three states mentioned above in respect of their own oppositions, Beijing has accused the Uyghurs of Islamic extremism, among other charges. Indeed, there have been reports that some Chinese Uyghur elements have had contact with the Taliban and with Osama bin Ladin. Although the threat of creating an independent East Turkestan or Uyghur state, much less basing it on Islam, does not seem serious, the Shanghai Five (China, Russia, Kazakhstan, Kyrgyzstan and Tajikistan) have held

[28] Abdullaev, 'Islam i "islamskii faktor" v sovremennom Uzbekistane', p. 99.
[29] *Newsweek International*, 5 June 2000.
[30] For the implications of this threat for Russia's position in Central Asia, see *Turkistan Newsletter*, 22 June 2000.
[31] EIU Country Report, *Uzbekistan*, December 2000, pp. 8 and 14.

regular meetings to ensure mutual security and to stress their common interest in preserving the territorial status quo, particularly with regard to ethnic separatism and Islamic extremism. It was in this context that Beijing offered assistance to Central Asian states in the wake of IMU and other religious 'extremist' attacks in 1999 and 2000.[32] In June 2001 Uzbekistan joined the Shanghai Five, which now became the Shanghai Cooperation Organization and opened its ranks to other appropriate candidates. The charter and regulations of the new organization were to be elaborated by the next summit in summer 2002.

Considerable hopes were placed by the Muslim successor states on membership of Muslim international organizations, the most important being the Islamic Conference Organization (ICO) and the Economic Cooperation Organization (ECO). In December 1991 Iran sponsored a proposal for admitting the newly independent Muslim states to the ICO and, hosting the ECO two months later, it sought to extend ECO membership to them. All six states duly joined, some of them after a period of deliberation. ICO membership offers access to the Islamic Development Bank, which has pledged financial support and technical assistance for ECO initiatives, including educational ones, many of which are meant for the CIS states. Founded in 1972 as a political institution to promote cooperation among Muslim states, the ICO is, in the words of one scholar, 'an Islamic institution, and may be considered an Islamist one in the conservative and limited sense of being committed to promoting Islamic causes'. Its charter includes among its objectives promoting 'Islamic solidarity' among member states; coordinating efforts 'for the safeguarding of the Holy Places and support of the people of Palestine'; and strengthening 'the struggle of all Muslim peoples with a view to safeguarding their dignity, independence and national rights'. On the whole, however, the organization 'has not pursued any active policy towards the Muslim CIS states or achieved a high profile in the region'. It has occasionally affirmed support for Azerbaijan's territorial integrity, although neither frequently nor effectively enough to satisfy the Azerbaijanis. On the other hand, it refrained from strong criticism of Russia during the first Chechen war and refused Chechnya's application for membership.[33]

---

[32] For the background to the situation in and around Xinjiang, see Sean R. Roberts, 'The Uigurs of the Kazakstan Borderlands: Migration and the Nation', *Nationalities Papers*, September 1998, vol. 26, no. 3, pp. 511–30; and Witt Rajcka, 'Xinjiang and its Central Asian Borderlands', *Central Asian Survey,* September 1998, vol. 17, no. 3, pp. 373–407. For more recent developments, see *Turkistan Newsletter*, 10 and 22 December 1999 and 31 March 2000; *Central Asia: Islamist Mobilisation and Regional Security*, pp. 25–6; and Andenov Marat, 'Ekstremisty v Tsentral'no-Aziatskom regione. Real'no?', *APR*, 3 September 2000.

[33] Herzig, 'Islam, Transnationalism and Subregionalism', pp. 247–8. According to Herzig (ibid., p. 248), the clearest expression of the ECO's Muslim character is its membership – it is the successor to the non-functioning Regional Cooperation Development (RCD) which was created in 1964 and comprised Iran, Turkey and Pakistan. Tehran viewed the inclusion of the Muslim successor states as a step towards an Islamic economic and political alliance. Menashri, 'Iran and Central Asia', p. 85.

On a different level, some of the CIS's Islamic parties and movements are affiliated with international associations or organizations. One of these is Hizb al-Tahrir al-Islami (see Chapter 4). It is not at all clear how far its branches in Uzbekistan and Tajikistan enjoy or can attain autonomy or independence from the central body, from which it receives its ideology and propaganda materials.

Islamic solidarity both within the CIS and with states outside it has been far less significant than some had hoped in the early 1990s and than others have continued to fear. At the same time, it must not be totally ignored, as it clearly has a potential that in certain circumstances could take practical form. Islam's radicalization in the CIS has had its roots in local and regional processes, notably the social transformation that has accompanied the formation of the USSR's successor states, but foreign Islamic involvement has been a catalyst to it. This involvement has complicated the already difficult relations between Islam at the local level and the Muslim CIS governments, and in certain instances it has had a significant impact on the evolution of local Islam.

8 UNDER WHAT CIRCUMSTANCES MIGHT ISLAM THREATEN STABILITY?

The previous chapters provide indications of what may be in store in the more intensely Islamic areas of the CIS unless radical changes occur in the population's social circumstances and in government policy in the relevant states. The questions that need to be posed in this context are the following: in what sense do Islamists constitute a significant threat to the stability and even existence of the current regimes or, alternatively, to society in various states of the CIS? Is an Islamic state likely to be set up anywhere in the CIS, and if so, where and in what circumstances? What, if anything, can be done to divert Islamic radicalism towards compromise and negotiation and away from confrontation and resorting to violence? A review of the events and developments of the years 1999 and 2000 may give an edge to these questions and help in finding some answers.

The lessons of Tashkent, February 1999

The Uzbek government took increasingly repressive measures against Islamic 'extremists' in the course of 1998 (see Chapter 6). When, on 16 February 1999, a number of bombs were detonated in the centre of Tashkent and killed sixteen people, President Karimov appeared on television and announced that extremist forces in Afghanistan had been contemplating the establishment of an Islamic state in Uzbekistan since its independence. He compared the security and stability in Uzbekistan with the chaos, disorder and loss of life in neighbouring Tajikistan and Afghanistan and accused the perpetrators of the bomb attacks of desiring to 'instil disarray in the hearts of people'. They hoped, according to Karimov, to deter foreign investors, shatter the aspirations of the younger generation and weaken the people's trust in his government's policy. Referring to those imprisoned in the past year (see Chapter 6), Karimov sought to differentiate between those who had instigated the events in the Fergana Valley and who had been trained abroad and received arms, instructions and dollars and those who had been led astray, whom he was ready to amnesty. The imams (prayer-leaders) in the mosques, Karimov insisted, should be protecting people's spiritual values, disseminating Islam and the *suras* of the Qur'an, and warning people and opening their eyes rather than indulging in empty talk. The *mahalla* councils should supervise the local mosques in order to ensure that the imams were fulfilling their duties – improving the life of the neighbourhood and inculcating in people's minds the belief in life after death.[1] Both Uzbekistan's media and the president accused radical Islamic groups of perpetrating the bomb attacks, and at one point Karimov attributed them to 'imperial forces', namely Moscow.[2]

Opening parliament in April, Karimov said that 'certain forces outside Uzbekistan wish us to abandon the secular road', and that 'the enemies of peace and stability in Uzbekistan are using Islam as camouflage' in their attempts to 'interfere with our construction of a new democratic civilized state'. To achieve their end, they were prepared to use every means, including acts of terrorism. He announced that those accused in connection with the February bombings would go on trial in the following month. Lists obtained from 'reliable sources' gave over 150 names; all were charged with terrorism, belonging to illegal religious groups, endeavouring to overthrow the constitutional order in Uzbekistan and illegal possession of weapons and narcotics.[3]

The possibility cannot be ruled out that the February bombings in Tashkent, for which no organization took responsibility and which were a far more sophisticated operation than others initiated by the IMU, were provoked by the country's security services upon orders from the president in order to justify further arrests and repression of political opponents and religious figures who rejected the jurisdiction of the Islamic establishment. (It will be remembered in this context that many people in Russia believe that the explosions in a number of Russian cities in summer 1999[4] that gave Vladimir Putin a pretext to initiate the second Chechen war were instigated by him and the security forces.) The bombings in Tashkent certainly served this purpose and were given all possible publicity. The severe measures taken by the Karimov regime in the previous fifteen months (see Chapter 6) had aroused domestic disquiet and external protest, which caused Karimov considerable concern, especially because it threatened to affect adversely his country's prestige and to discourage foreign investment. It is also possible, however, that the bombings had another explanation, such as a 'turf war' over cotton or narcotics linked to regime infighting, or mafiosi or the president's rivals within his own administration putting out warning signals to Karimov.

At the first trial in May, of twenty-two men accused of involvement in the bombings, the picture that came to light corresponded very largely to that drawn by the Uzbek authorities in their immediate aftermath. All were found guilty, six being condemned to death and the others receiving long prison sentences. Nearly all the defendants said they first fell under the influence of Islam through a local religious figure, mostly a *qori* (one who recites the Qur'an in the mosque and elsewhere).

---

[1] *Turkistan Newsletter*, 24 February 1999.
[2] *Turkistan Newsletter*, 26 April 1999.
[3] *Turkistan Newsletter*, 20 May 1999.
[4] The reference is to explosions in apartment houses in Moscow, Volgodonsk in Rostov province and Buinaksk in Dagestan that led to some 300 deaths (see below, p. 77).

Some described the breadth and efficiency of the Islamic terrorist network. Not a few of the accused had been arrested in other countries (Kazakhstan, Kyrgyzstan, Tajikistan, Russia, Ukraine and Turkey) and handed over to the Uzbek government. Others had been arrested throughout Uzbekistan. Some spoke of meetings in southern Kazakhstan and even in Pavlodar in northern Kazakhstan. One man had gone to Turkey, where he had met with Tohir Yoldosh, who had sent him on missions to Azerbaijan, Chechnya, Cyprus, Iran and the United Arab Emirates. He brought back to Almaty religious literature, Islamic video cassettes and US dollars, as well as other money he received from Yoldosh and Mohammed Solih, the exiled leader of the secular nationalist opposition party Erk, all of which he handed on to Juma Namangani. Another defendant had trained with IMU forces in northern Afghanistan, and a third had received training in a special camp in Chechnya. One man, who claimed to have maintained constant contact with Yoldosh, said he had been assigned the task of recruiting young men and sending them for training in Tajikistan and Afghanistan.[5] The inclusion of Mohammed Solih in the testimonies – from the beginning Karimov had accused him of participation in the bombings – seems to strengthen the suggestion that the object of the trials (if not of the bombings) was to implicate all Karimov's opponents, not just those who were in fact Islamists.

Eighteen months later the Supreme Court of Uzbekistan passed verdict on twelve men clearly perceived to be the leaders of the opposition, all or most of whom were being tried *in absentia*. The court passed the death sentence on both Yoldosh and Namangani and sentenced the other ten defendants, including Mohammed Solih, to long prison terms (twelve to twenty years). The verdict emphasized the continuity in the activity of Yoldosh and Namangani from 1991 to 2000, their ultimate objective being to overturn the existing regime and replace it with an Islamic state. The sentence made several references to the IMU leadership's links with Tajikistan, where Namangani had established a military base; with Chechnya, where a number of the movement's members had gone for training; and with Afghanistan, Pakistan, and also Iran and Turkey.[6]

Batken, August–September 1999

At the very end of July 1999 a small group of Uzbek militants, members of the IMU who had taken refuge in Garm in eastern Tajikistan, undertook an armed incursion into Kyrgyzstan's Batken region. It has been suggested that the events in southern Kyrgyzstan in 1999 and 2000 (see below) should not be described as an incursion,

[5] Radio Free Europe/Radio Liberty (henceforth RFE/RL), 2 July 1999; and *Pravda vostoka*, 10 June 1999.
[6] *Pravda vostoka*, 23 November 2000.

many of those involved in them inhabiting the border region, 'moving back and forth, building arms caches, and establishing relations with the local villagers and even drawing recruits from among them'.[7] Their numbers were enhanced in the second half of August, reaching somewhere between 500 and 1,000. They took several villages, and a number of hostages, creating a tense situation in Kyrgyzstan and causing a deterioration of relations between it and Uzbekistan, which sent planes into Kyrgyzstan to attack the insurgents. They seem to have been forced out of Kyrgyzstan by October 1999.

In the early 1990s, Yoldosh and Namangani, the IMU's leaders, had fled Uzbekistan to Tajikistan. The ranks of their followers swelled as the Karimov regime tightened its hold and increased its repression of Islamic radicals, particularly from December 1997 (see Chapter 4). By May 1999, when a clash among their ranks brought them to the notice of the Tajik authorities, there were some 1,500 Uzbek refugees in Garm, the region in Tajikistan where the Islamic Revival Party of Tajikistan was traditionally the strongest. The Uzbek and Tajik governments reached an agreement in late July for their repatriation. As the refugees clearly feared what would befall them upon returning to Uzbekistan, they apparently decided to take drastic action, moving into Kyrgyzstan and declaring they would bring *jihad* to Uzbekistan.

By the time representatives of the security organizations of the three states concerned met towards the end of August, the Kyrgyz had been openly antagonized by the Uzbek bombing of their territory, as a result of which a number of civilians were killed and injured. (Uzbek planes also struck in those areas of Garm where the refugees had surfaced.) For his part, Karimov charged the Kyrgyz with not acting effectively to quell the incursion. Kyrgyzstan turned for assistance to Russia, whose Defence Minister, Igor Sergeev, flew to Tashkent for talks with the Uzbek government.[8] This was the first of several meetings between Russian and Central Asian leaders that eventually, in January 2000, led to an agreement between Russia and four of the five Central Asian states (Turkmenistan was the exception) to participate in joint military exercises on Uzbek and Kyrgyz territory. Given the recurrent tensions among the Central Asian states, only Russia could effectively ensure the requisite coordination that was a *sine qua non* for successful action against the Islamists. Simultaneously,

[7] Associated Press, 29 October 2000, quoted in *Central Asia: Islamist Mobilisation and Regional Security*, p. 19.

[8] RFE/RL, 31 August and 1 September 1999. According to this source the 1,500 refugees included families. Another source, however, claimed that a representative of the UN Commission for Refugees in Tajikistan said there were 1,500 fighting personnel. O. Bibikova, 'Blizhnee zarubezh'e', *Aziia i Afrika segodnia*, no. 2, 2000, p. 16. A year later Russian Defence Minister Sergeev contended there were up to 5,000 militants in the IMU, some of whom were still training in Afghanistan – Marat Mamadshoyev, 'The Central Asian Insurgency Raises Questions about Civilian Sympathies and Military Capabilities', *Eurasia Insight*, 25 August 2000. For the background to the worsening relations between Kyrgyzstan and Uzbekistan, see *Turkistan Newsletter*, 27 January 2000.

the twelve members of the CIS agreed to draft a security programme to fight terrorism and religious extremism, including apparently the establishment in the CIS of an international anti-terrorist centre.[9] Clearly the main beneficiary of the Batken affair was Russia, for it underscored Uzbekistan's need for Russian aid and meant its return to the fold.[10] Batken enabled President Putin to take a major step towards reviving Russia's role as a dominant power without which the other Soviet successor states were manifestly incapable of solving urgent security issues.

The second Chechen war

Russia's ignominious retreat from the first Chechen war (see Chapter 4) left its military establishment smarting. A series of incidents in August–September 1999 provided a pretext for Moscow to renew its repression of the Chechens and to try to put an end for all time to Chechen claims to independence. The incidents began with the incursion into Dagestan of a force of some 2,000 men led by two Chechen 'warlords', Shamil Basayev and Emir Khattab, in coordination with radical elements within the Islamic Jamaat of Dagestan, and the seizure of a number of Dagestani villages, where they hoped to create an Islamic polity more significant than the territory that had been functioning under Salafi control since May 1998 (see Chapter 5). The spokesman of the Islamists said their ultimate aim was to separate the North Caucasus from Russia and bring it under Islamic rule.[11] The second stage was a series of explosions in apartment buildings in several Russian cities which caused the death of approximately 300 civilians and which the Russian government officially attributed to Chechen terrorists.

Although the main issue of contention between Moscow and Grozny since 1991 had been the status of Chechnya and its relationship to the Russian Federation, the Russian federal government sought to portray its confrontation with the Chechens primarily as a fight against Islamic extremism and terror. President Dudayev had on the whole refrained from Islamic rhetoric during the first Chechen war, but the second war was heavily cloaked in Islamic terms. This time the Chechen leadership declared *jihad* against Russia, and Chechen fighters referred to themselves as *mujahidin* (the term used by the Afghan opposition to the Marxist regime that came to power in 1978). According to one scholar, Islam was particularly attractive to fatalistic soldiers in the context of the country's total devastation and the death of close to 50,000 people. A religiously defined conflict, he points out further, entailed a significantly

---

[9] RFE/RL, 25 and 26 January 2000.
[10] For Uzbekistan's defection in 1998, see Chapter 6.
[11] *Turkistan Newsletter*, 13 and 16 September 1999. For a detailed study and analysis of the developments that led to the démarche of August 1999, see Makarov, *Ofitsial'nyi i neofitsial'nyi islam v Dagestane*, pp. 39–65.

greater risk of overspill than the ethnically defined one of 1994–6. Although the likelihood of outright rebellion in other parts of the North Caucasus remained small, the Islamic revival in those areas did mean a decline in their populations' loyalty to Moscow and in Russian control, especially as there were indications that several hundred members of other North Caucasian peoples were fighting with the Chechens. It is not clear whether the 1,500 volunteers the Russian government claimed to have intercepted at the Ukrainian border on the way to Chechnya and the further 400 who Moscow said had tried to enter Chechnya from Georgia came from other parts of the CIS or from abroad. Zelimkhan Yandarbiyev went on a fund-raising tour of Pakistan in February 2000, with considerable success, and Chechnya opened a diplomatic mission in Kabul a month previously. Undoubtedly, both sides had an interest in inflating figures of volunteers – the Chechens in order to boost morale and the Russians to highlight that they were waging a struggle against 'global Islamic terrorism', but the fact of external assistance of various kinds seemed undeniable, and meant that the consequences of a Russian failure in this second round would probably be much more serious than in 1996.[12]

The second Batken crisis and the incursion into Uzbekistan, August 2000

On 7 August 2000 clashes with IMU insurgents occurred in the mountainous area of Surkhandarya in southern Uzbekistan. (There were different versions regarding how long IMU militants had been in the region before the outbreak of fighting.[13] It is possible that some might have infiltrated into Uzbekistan from Kyrgyzstan during the Batken crisis in summer 1999 and remained – in addition to those involved in the Angren incident in November 1999.[14]) Within a week or so the fighting spread to Kyrgyzstan. The tactics employed in summer 2000 differed from those of the previous year. In the first place, rather than mounting a major attack, the IMU now preferred to make incursions by small groups, usually of up to 100 men, although on the night of 1–2

---

[12] Svante E. Cornell, 'Cloaking the Chechen War as Jihad: The Risk of Military Contagion', *Turkistan Newsletter*, 22 June 2000; *Newsweek International*, 13 March 2000. Among other charges, Russia claimed that bin Ladin had provided the Chechens with $250 million and sent some 150 armed men from Afghanistan in response to a request from Emir Khattab.

[13] Andenov Marat, 'Ekstremisty v Tsentral'no-Aziatskom regione. Real'no?', *APR*, 3 September 2000.

[14] This incident involved a shoot-out between Uzbek troops led by Interior Minister Zakir Almatov and a handful of insurgents in Yangiabad district, near Angren in Tashkent province. Speaking about the incident, President Karimov noted that one of the militants was a resident of Dagestan, from which he inferred the connection between terrorism in Central Asia and North Caucasus. He also took the opportunity to criticize the Kyrgyz government, whose 'weak policy' was the cause of 'these things' happening. Uzbek TV, 17 November 1999, monitored by the BBC. (I am grateful to Adiba Ataeva of the BBC for this information.)

September a larger, three-pronged attack by 240 men occurred in Batken. Secondly, IMU forces attacked villages and military posts over a much larger area. On 22 August a group of gunmen even attacked a police post in Tashkent province. The IMU's demands to the Uzbek government, announced on 14 August, included the release of all IMU members imprisoned in Uzbekistan, the re-opening of all mosques shut down by the Uzbek government, the sanctioning of Muslim dress and the imposition of *Shari'a* law.[15] According to Human Rights Watch, the fighting displaced over 1,000 civilians, and dozens of Uzbek and Kyrgyz government troops reportedly were killed. On 14 August the Kyrgyz, Tajiks and Uzbeks established a joint headquarters in Tajikistan's Leninabad/Sugd region in order to coordinate their response, and on 20 August the leaders of these three states and Kazakhstan met in Bishkek with the Russian Security Council Secretary, Sergei Ivanov, and published a statement committing their governments to 'the most decisive measures' to crush 'terrorist actions'.[16] Once again there were recriminations among the governments concerned: the Uzbeks and the Kyrgyz insisted that the fighters entered their territory from Tajikistan and criticized Tajikistan for letting the IMU use its space to cross into their respective countries; the Tajiks denied these allegations.[17] The secretary of Kyrgyzstan's Security Council claimed that the incursion had been financed by international terrorist organizations backed by Osama bin Ladin and that it was designed to destabilize Central Asia and to increase the drug traffic from Afghanistan. He specifically linked Namangani's name with the narcotics trade.[18] Indications that the IMU and other radical Muslim organizations and groups in the North Caucasus and Central Asia have ties with the narcotics trade which has flourished in Central Asia and the Russian Federation since the break-up of the USSR and even with international drug traffickers have not been proved beyond doubt. Allusions to such connections clearly serve to win favour at home and abroad for the regimes' endeavours to repress Islamic 'extremists', and that was the rationale behind statements that Islamists had narcotics in their possession and had been arrested on that score (see Chapter 6 and above).

Although the official Central Asian media were tight-lipped about the attitude of the local civilian population to the insurgents, there were indications that at least some demonstrated their sympathy and provided them with food supplies.[19] According

[15] RFE/RL, 23 August 2000; International Crisis Group, *Central Asia Briefing*, 18 October 2000, pp. 4–5.

[16] *Eurasia Insight*, 23 August 2000; and *Central Asia Briefing*, 18 October 2000, p. 11.

[17] *Eurasia Insight*, 25 August 2000, and RFE/RL, 1 September 2000.

[18] Turat Akimov, 'Kogda zakonchitsia vtoraia Batkenskaia voina?', *APR*, 3 September 2000.

[19] According to at least one source, the incursion into Batken in 1999 had also encountered the support and sympathy of the local population. Ashimbaev and Shomanov, 'Politizatsiia islama na postsovetskom prostranstve', p. 113. For the version that local villagers had actually joined the fighters in 1999, see above.

to human rights activists such support was the result of a combination of repressive government policies and widespread poverty. Yet not all civilians favoured the insurgents, who resorted to burning two villages about 60 miles from Tashkent after their residents had refused to welcome them.

The government forces of Uzbekistan and Kyrgyzstan seem to have been singularly unsuccessful in containing the IMU fighters. President Karimov admitted that they had at first been unprepared – a rather lame confession in view of the 1999 incursion and the subsequent decision to conduct joint manoeuvres in the area. The use of aircraft and artillery once again proved to be of limited value, given the mountainous terrain, which provided the insurgents with ample cover. In mid-October, over two months after the first incursion, efforts by Kyrgyzstan's armed forces to expel the remaining insurgents were still continuing.[20] Russian military officials attributed the ineffectiveness of the Central Asian armed forces to lack of coordination among them.[21]

Once again, Karimov seems to have handled the situation in a way designed to strengthen his and Uzbekistan's image in Moscow and Washington as a natural barrier to the spread of radical Islamism and to justify the military aid he has received from both. In September 2000 Washington declared the IMU to be a terrorist organization, after concluding that it had links with Osama bin Laden.[22] On the other hand, however, Karimov criticized what he described as Moscow's exaggeration of the threat of Islamic fundamentalism in Central Asia.[23] In the domestic arena it appears that the president's authoritarianism, the absence of political reform and the economic crisis have undermined support for him and swelled the ranks of the opposition, also radicalizing it and enhancing its Islamic character. While authoritarianism may strengthen Karimov in the short run, the ineffectiveness of his repression in eradicating the cause of discontent and silencing the Islamists will almost certainly engender instability in the medium and long term.[24] One study, which based its findings on rather extensive fieldwork, contends that support for Karimov has been declining, especially among the middle class, dissatisfied with economic performance, and moderate Islamists, estranged on the one hand by the subordination of official Islam to the regime, and on the other hand by the arbitrary persecution of rank-and-file Muslims.[25]

[20] *Central Asia Briefing*, 18 October 2000, p. 14.

[21] *Eurasia Insight*, 25 August 2000.

[22] EIU Country Report, *Uzbekistan*, December 2000, p. 13. According to this same source, Germany and China too have offered aid to Uzbekistan in the context of its struggle against the IMU and Islamic radicalism.

[23] *Rossiiskaia gazeta*, 10 October 2000. This criticism is to be seen in the light of Putin's threats against Afghanistan and Karimov's contacts with the Taliban. See Chapter 7.

[24] See, for instance, Reuel Hanks, 'The "Fundamentalist" Threat to Uzbekistan: Crisis or Chimera?', *Central Asia-Caucasus Analyst*, 30 August 2000; *Turkistan Newsletter*, 20 November 2000.

[25] *Central Asia: Islamist Mobilisation and Regional Security*, pp. 15–18.

Summary

The events of 1999–2000 brought to a head trends that had been manifest for some years. Among them was an escalation of acts of terror (in Tashkent in February 1999 and in a number of Russian cities in the summer of the same year). Although there was no solid proof of a connection between these bombings and radical Islamic groups, the Uzbek and Russian governments were prompt to highlight the 'manifest' nature of this link. The political benefits they sought to gain from playing up a link aroused suspicions regarding its authenticity. Vladimir Putin, indeed, launched his presidential career with the second Chechen war, which was allegedly intended to cut the North Caucasians, particularly the Chechens, down to size and guarantee the security of Russia's citizens.

The cynicism of the leadership of Russia and the Muslim successor states in flaunting the Islamic threat to stability, law and order so as to justify their own tendency to outright authoritarianism has exposed the chasm between the stability of society and the durability of regimes. Putin, Karimov and their counterparts have made every effort to indicate that the two are synonymous and that radical Islam poses a threat to both. Careful analysis of the events described in this chapter casts serious doubt on both contentions. Concerning the overlap between, not to speak of the identity of, society and regime, the mass arrests in Uzbekistan suggested instead the unsettling social consequences of the line pursued by the Uzbek government. The same can be argued about Russia, as it becomes increasingly clear that despite the great devastation inflicted by the Russian army in Chechnya, a total defeat of the Chechen 'opposition' has not been achieved and that the war is still likely to demand considerable sacrifice of Russian lives. As for the threat of radical Islam to regimes, it is doubtful that it is a direct one. None of the various radical Islamic organizations look like organizing in such a way as to be able to usurp power. They have shown themselves to be limited in leadership, organizational ability, finances and even determination. Where there have been resolute and well-trained Islamists, their Islamism has been subordinate to other features, except again in the case of the small force that sought in 1999 to create a mini-Islamistan in northwest Dagestan. Radical Islam has, however, damaged the credibility of regimes which have prided themselves on their ability to impose and preserve order, and has contributed to a sense of insecurity. This, in turn, has interfered with social and economic development, strengthened undemocratic tendencies and fostered conditions for corruption and drug-trafficking. In this sense, radical Islam would seem to unleash forces that might in certain circumstances provide a major challenge to the powers-that-be. The greatest risk created by the events of 1999 and 2000 is that they might become identified with wide popular aspirations for better economic conditions and a more Islamic society.[26]

[26] Ibid., p. 23.

Although all other radical opposition groups have been effectively quelled, Islamic ones have been more difficult to repress. This is a consequence apparently of their sense of conviction that they are pursuing a mission in fighting the infidel, whether Russian or national apostate; of the external support they garner; and, perhaps most importantly, of the sympathy they evoke among elements of the population, from which their ranks are constantly replenished. In the event of a dramatic event such as the demise of a head of government, Islamic groups may well seek to present an alternative to the official successor.

Almost by the same token, the argument that radical Islam might present a threat to the stability of society seems quite far-fetched. Society at large perceives Islam as part of its collective identity, an integral component of its ethnic culture and tradition. For the majority in most areas Islam seems to be tacit or latent, and they are unlikely to credit regime propaganda – even if it is transmitted through the religious establishment – that Islam in any form presents a danger to their well-being. At the same time, except in relatively small pockets, such as parts of Uzbekistan's Fergana Valley, Karategin in Tajikistan and a few mountain villages in Dagestan, the population as a whole seems unlikely to identify actively with radical, political Islam. Not only the urban intelligentsia but also rural populations have made it clear that their main interest lies in ameliorating their economic position, not in mounting the barricades in the name of Islam. The more the radical Islamists have shown a readiness to introduce their own norms of behaviour, the less popular they became. This has apparently been less the result of regime propaganda than of the lessons learned from the partial successes of the Islamists in, for example, Tajikistan and Dagestan. In Tajikistan, the population seems to believe that the IRPT was to blame for the outbreak of civil war that rent the country for some five years (see Chapter 4). In Dagestan, in the face of the success of the Salafis, Sufis took over the republican spiritual administration and eventually joined hands with the republican secular authority (see Chapter 5).

9 CONCLUSION

The politicization of Islam has been a feature of the last half-century or so in different parts of the Muslim world, particularly where it has been accompanied by a struggle for independence from colonial rule and social and economic hardship. In view of globalization, no region of the Muslim world can be arbitrarily or artificially cut off from this process. In states where no genuine opposition is allowed to take official form and Islam has no political outlet or expression within a parliamentary framework, its political message must necessarily adopt an antagonistic, anti-government, anti-establishment stance. In other words, political Islam becomes, willy-nilly, antithetical to the wider interests of the state and an enemy of its leadership, though not necessarily of the community as a whole.[1]

At the same time, the Muslim ethnic groups of the CIS have been experiencing a general Islamic revival. Those members, particularly young adults, who have taken Islam seriously and absorbed the message their Islamic mentors have sought to convey, have felt frustrated by the secular, 'modernizing' goals the leaders of their respective states have set for them. With their standard of living steadily plummeting and unemployment rife, they have naturally turned to political Islam as the sole ostensible solution to their grievances. As one commentator has noted, in an Islamic culture Islamic vocabulary and symbolism can naturally be effective, because their 'sense of timeliness and weight' results from political and economic conditions 'in combination with the deliberate policies of repressive elites'.[2] Also, it seems certain that Islamic radicalism is strongest in poor rural areas, and at least some officials in the Muslim states concur that it may have economic roots.[3] Be this as it may, in the year 2000 nearly one-half of the Muslims of Uzbekistan and Kazakhstan were of the

---

[1] For discussion of these issues, see, for example, Martin Kramer (ed.), *The Islamism Debate* (Tel Aviv: The Moshe Dayan Center for Middle Eastern and African Studies, Tel Aviv University, 1997); Olivier Roy, *The Failure of Political Islam* (Cambridge, MA: Harvard University Press, 1994); and Bassam Tibi, *The Challenge of Fundamentalism: Political Islam and the New World Disorder* (Berkeley, CA: University of California Press, 1998).

[2] Richard Foltz, 'Islam and Identity in Post-Soviet Central Asia: Some Historical Considerations', *The Harriman Review*, vol. 11, no. 3, April 1999, p. 43.

[3] *The Uzbekistan Report*, 2 January 2001, *www.uzreport.com/cg*, quoted the Kazakhstan Security Council secretary as doubting, given this situation, whether military measures such as closing state borders would be effective.

opinion that Islam should play a major role in their country's political life.[4] In this way, the intransigence towards political Islam of the governments concerned has been self-defeating. In a sense, their warnings about the dangers of subversion on the part of Islamic extremists and fundamentalists have been a self-fulfilling prophecy.

At the time of writing (mid-2001) there seems to be no way that Islamic parties and movements can be contained or subdued in the long term. Their persistent repression by hardline regimes has served no purpose, except perhaps to make their intransigence more resolute. As long as they are not co-opted into the system by the creation of a civil society in which they can play an appropriate role within the consensus, they will continue to present a threat to the security of the regimes. This is not the threat that governments have been portraying; rather, it is the threat of major social undercurrents for which political Islam is the only feasible means of conveying dissatisfaction. Political Islam is, moreover, a medium that is particularly suitable to the prevalent circumstances in most CIS countries. This is because radical Islam tends to be obdurate and immune to extraneous influences in that it represents, or claims to represent, a religious ideology that cannot be bought out by governments and corrupted or bribed into accommodation.

It is the creation of a civil society rather than radical Islam that is likely to threaten the relevant regimes. As it would clearly be inexpedient to admit this, they prefer to seek legitimacy for their policies by pointing an accusing finger at Islam. But in doing so they actually enhance the political potential of the various Islamic oppositions. Were they to take the risk of bringing them into the political consensus, however, the chances of a radical Islamization of the societies in question would seem to be slight. In the first place, it seems highly implausible that the Islamists would remain united in view of not only traditional clan, tribal and regional rivalries between individual leaders but also irreconcilable religious differences. Secondly, were it to become an actual issue, many people – probably the overwhelming majority, even in the more devoutly Islamic regions – would not opt for the creation of an Islamic state. In contrast to the high percentage of respondents in Uzbekistan and Kazakhstan who thought Islam should play a major role in political life, in the one country where it has done so, Tajikistan, the figure was just 27 per cent. Those desirous of the rule of the *Shari'a* as against secular law are only a small minority.[5] Indeed, the various parties and movements in question would probably split over this very question.

Rather than relying on conflicts among the Muslim radicals, the governments and ruling elites of the countries under study need to change tack. Blaming each other for

---

[4] 'Central Asians Differ on Islam's Political Role', pp. 3–4, Figure 3 and Table 11. Interestingly, the figure for Kazakhstan was down from 66 per cent in 1997. (The figure for Azerbaijan was 21 per cent.)
[5] Ibid., p. 5, Figure 5 and Table 13. Those favouring religious rather than secular law comprised just 6 and 7 per cent of Muslims in Azerbaijan and Tajikistan respectively, 10 per cent in Uzbekistan and 19 per cent in Kazakhstan in the year 2000.

84

local conflagrations and accusing political opponents of subversion are not recommended remedies for a complex and charged situation. The Kazakh ethnographer and political analyst Nurbulat Masanov seems much nearer the mark when he identifies the regimes in power as the direct cause of regional instability; and although he is referring to Central Asia, undoubtedly the same applies to the North Caucasus. 'Violent confrontation', in his view, is bred not by Islam but by the 'decrease in democratic values' in all the states in question and 'the concentration of power in one set of hands'.[6]

---

[6] Masanov was speaking at a conference organized in Almaty by the Institute for War and Peace Reporting. IWPR's *Reporting Central Asia*, no. 29, 10 November 2000.

FURTHER READING

Bobrovnikov, Vladimir, 'Islamophobia and Religious Legislation in Daghestan', *Central Asia and the Caucasus*, no. 2, 2000, pp. 138–50.

Bohr, Annette, *Uzbekistan: Politics and Foreign Policy* (London: The Royal Institute of International Affairs, 1998).

Herzig, Edmund, 'Islam, Transnationalism and Subregionalism in the CIS', in Renata Dwan and Oleksandr Pavliuk (eds), *Building Security in the New States of Eurasia* (Armonk, NY: East-West Institute and M. E. Sharpe, 2000), pp. 227–57.

Jonson, Lena and Esenov, Murad (eds), *Political Islam and Conflicts in Russia and Central Asia* (Stockholm: The Swedish Institute of International Affairs, 1999).

Kisriev, Enver and Ware, Robert Bruce, 'The Islamic Factor in Dagestan', *Central Asian Survey*, vol. 19, no. 2, June 2000, pp. 235–52.

Sagdeev, Roald and Eisenhower, Susan (eds), *Islam and Central Asia: An Enduring Legacy or an Evolving Threat?* (Washington, DC: Center for Political and Strategic Studies, 2000).

Yemelianova, Galina M., 'Islam and Nation Building in Tatarstan and Dagestan in the Russian Federation', *Nationalities Papers*, vol. 27, no. 4, December 1999, pp. 605–30.

Related titles in the
Central Asian and Caucasian Prospects series

Philip Micklin *Managing Water in Central Asia*

An evaluation of the use of water by the Central Asian states. The paper discusses water resource geography along with other critical water issues including irrigated agriculture, the Aral Sea problem, water sharing among the Aral Sea basin states, national water politics, and the future of water management. These management issues are central to understanding and tackling the environmental and agricultural challenges confronting Central Asia, and also have the potential to generate conflicts both within and between states.

Richard Pomfret *Central Asia Turns South? Trade Relations in Transition*

The author examines the trade relations of the Central Asian states with Turkey, Iran, Pakistan, and Afghanistan. He assesses the Soviet economic and trade legacy in the region as well as the relevant physical infrastructure. He analyses the policy environment, outlines trade patterns, and considers the prospects for greater regional integration.

Neil MacFarlane *Western Engagement in the Caucasus and Central Asia*

This paper analyses Western political and economic engagement in the Caucasus and Central Asia and explores the issue of how such involvement shaped developments in the countries of the region in terms of their internal politics, their values and the orientations they assumed. The extent to which Western engagement has influenced economic and security policy-making in the region is also addressed.

ORDERING INFORMATION

UK and Rest of Europe	US, Canada and Rest of World
Plymbridge Distributors	The Brookings Institution Press
Tel (+44) 01752 202301	Tel 1 800 275 1447 or 797 202 6258
Fax (+44) 01752 202333	Fax 202 797 2960

Central Asian Security:
The New International Context
Lena Jonson and Roy Allison (eds)

This volume is the first comprehensive scholarly analysis of the strategic recon-
figuration of Central Asia as Russia has become more disengaged from the CIS states
in the region and they have developed new relations to the south, east and west. It
assesses a variety of internal security policy challenges confronting these states and
examines the security policy relevance of their expanding network of relations with
regional and international powers – Russia, Turkey, Iran, China and the United States.
Internal challenges and the evolution of relations with external powers may result in
new cooperative relationships but may also lead to destabilizing rivalry and interstate
enmity in Central Asia. It is important to identify new patterns of relevance for future
security cooperation in the region, but the potential for a new security system or for
new institutions to manage security in the region remains uncertain. These issues are
explored by a team of prominent specialists from Western Europe, the United States,
Russia and China.

'Readable, authoritative and comprehensive ... the best analysis of its kind on the
security issues facing Central Asia'—*International Affairs*

Brookings/RIIA, April 2001
ISBN 0 8157 0105 5 (paper) £16.95
296 pp

ORDERING INFORMATION

UK and Rest of Europe
Plymbridge Distributors
Tel (+44) 01752 202301
Fax (+44) 01752 202333

US, Canada and Rest of World
The Brookings Institution Press
Tel 1 800 275 1447 or 797 202 6258
Fax 202 797 2960